A JOURNALIST'S GUIDE TO THE INTERNET

The Net as a Reporting Tool

CHRISTOPHER CALLAHAN

Arizona State University

LESLIE-JEAN THORNTON

Arizona State University

PEARSON

Boston ■ New York ■ San Francisco ■ Mexico City ■ Montreal ■ Toronto ■ London ■ Madrid ■ Munich ■ Paris Hong Kong ■ Singapore ■ Tokyo ■ Cape Town ■ Sydney

ISBN 13: 978-0-205-56595-5
ISBN 10: 0-205-56595-6

Printed in the United States of America
10 9 8 7 6 5 4 3 2 1   11 10 9 8 07

CONTENTS

PREFACE

The Internet has changed dramatically since the publication of the first edition of *A Journalist's Guide to the Internet* eight years ago. According to NUA. com, a company that tracks Internet demographics and trends, the number of global Internet users had more than tripled between the first and second publication of this book—from 150 million in December 1998 to 513.4 million by August 2001. Numerous sources say the 1 billion mark was passed in 2005, and Internet World Stats reported more than 1.1 billion users in July 2007. By the end of 2005 in the United States alone, some 200 million people were Internet users. The Pew Internet & American Life 2005 survey found 94 million of them were online every day. An estimated 77 percent of the U.S. population was online by fall 2006 compared to barely 25 percent when the first edition was released. Internet access in the newsroom is the norm today, a far cry from the situation eight years ago.

But the extraordinary growth of the Internet has not fundamentally changed the extraordinary possibilities—and very dangerous pitfalls—of the Internet that we discussed in the first edition. It has only magnified both aspects, making the Net more useful and, at the same time, more dangerous to journalists. The Internet—with its instant and mostly free access to millions of data sources around the world—provides reporters and editors with the most important journalistic tool since the telephone. But when used poorly, the Internet can be detrimental to journalism by increasing sloppy and inaccurate reporting. In short, the Internet almost always will make good reporters better, and usually will make bad reporters worse. Same for editors. The mission of this updated edition is the same as previous editions: to provide a road map to help good journalists make their journalism better.

The tone of the book, we hope, also remains the same. It is a book, first and foremost, about journalism, not computers. That is a critical distinction in understanding and using the text. Amazon.com lists nearly a half million computer books available, with thousands on the Internet alone.*

This book looks at the Internet from a *journalistic* perspective: How best can reporters and editors, facing tight and unbending deadlines, use this technology accurately and efficiently to improve the quality of their journalism?

In Chapter 1, we look at how to think strategically about the Internet, from the perspective of reporters and editors under deadline. Chapter 2 looks at how to evaluate the reliability of Internet-accessed information through a journalistic prism. Chapter 3 discusses the proliferation of rumors and misinformation on the Internet and how those untruths easily slip into

*The Library of Congress listed 2,124 titles—books and periodicals—under the subject heading "Internet" in early July 2007.

our news reports. The next three chapters detail some of the best Internet sites for journalists: basic resources, references and reporters' tools are in Chapter 4, top data sites make up Chapter 5, and Chapter 6 looks at online news publications. In Chapter 7, we discuss targeted search strategies, and Chapter 8 describes how to build a system of Internet sites specific to news beats. Chapter 9 shows how e-mail can be used to mine information automatically. An expanded Chapter 10 covers discussion groups, e-mail lists and newsgroups. A new Chapter 11 discusses the opportunities and challenges of using blogs as information sources and lists more than a hundred blogs journalists should know about. The final chapter shows how the Internet can be useful to journalists trying to improve their craft, keep up on new developments in the profession, or find their next jobs. As before, some of the nation's best journalists tell their favorite stories to illustrate how the Net has worked for them.

This latest version of the book has been updated throughout to bring you the most current tools for your newsgathering. There's information on wikis, news aggregators, RSS feeds, social network sites, map and video searches, Webcams and mashups. We've described tools, such as ways to easily save Web pages and clips, which make organizing data easier. The reference guides have been expanded to reflect the global context of journalism today. *A Journalist's Guide to the Internet* is written as a practical, jargon-free guide. We hope you find it useful time and time again.

ACKNOWLEDGMENTS

This book is possible because of the generous time and energy spent by many colleagues around the country. We would especially like to thank Sarah Cohen of Investigative Reporters and Editors, Inc., and the *Washington Post,* Bill Dedman, Linda Fibich of the Newhouse News Source, Jeff Friedson of The Prudential, Chris Harvey of the University of Maryland, Linda Johnson of the *Lexington Herald-Leader,* Jennifer LaFleur of the *St. Louis Post-Dispatch,* Carl Sessions Stepp of the University of Maryland, and Mitchell Zuckoff of the *Boston Globe.* Each offered invaluable suggestions, guidance, and support.

We owe a special debt of gratitude to the journalists who generously contributed essays: Carl Cannon of the *National Journal,* Jo Craven of *Newsday,* Steven Eisenstadt, Phineas Fiske of *Newsday,* Penny Loeb of *U.S. News & World Report,* Bill Loving of the *Los Angeles Times,* David Milliron of the *Atlanta Journal-Constitution,* Heather Newman of the *Detroit Free Press,* Paul Overberg of *USA Today,* Neil Reisner of the *Dade Business Review,* Mark Schleif-Stein of the New Orleans *Times-Picayune,* Ernie Slone of the *Orange County Register,* Frank Sweeney of the *San Jose Mercury News,* and Duff Wilson of the *Seattle Times.*

Kelly McInerney and Chet Rhodes were responsible for showing me the power and potential of the Internet long before it became an integral part of our culture. Chris Harvey urged me to write the book in the first place. The reviewers—Judi Cook, Salem State College; Rebecca Dumlao, East Carolina University; R. Thomas Berner, The Pennsylvania State University; Keith Cannon, Wingate University; and Paul Husslebee, Southern Utah University—provided valuable comments. And of course, my ever-patient wife, Jeanmarie, through her encouragement and support, helped me see the project through.

—Christopher Callahan

We also wish to thank our colleagues at the Walter Cronkite School of Journalism at Arizona State University for their support during this updated edition. In particular, Sasan Pourepetezadi and Millie Christensen kept the information flowing in the most helpful ways. Jenny Lupica of Allyn and Bacon kept track of it all from Boston, and my husband, Randy Jessee, wisely answered journalism as well as computer questions from both sides of the country, as usual.

—Leslie-Jean Thornton

Christopher Callahan is the founding dean of the Walter Cronkite School of Journalism and Mass Communication at Arizona State University. He is a former Washington correspondent for The Associated Press. He also worked in AP bureaus in Boston, Providence, Augusta, Maine, and Concord, New Hampshire. He specialized in political and government coverage. Callahan is a graduate of Harvard University's John F. Kennedy School of Government and Boston University's School of Public Communication.

A Journalist's Guide to the Internet is an outgrowth of Callahan's research into practical uses of the Internet for reporters and editors on deadline. He has delivered seminars and workshops on the Internet for a wide variety of professional journalists and journalism organizations, including Investigative Reporters and Editors, the Society of Professional Journalists, *USA Today,* The Associated Press, the National Institute for Computer-Assisted Reporting, Voice of America, the National Conference of Editorial Writers, the Maryland-Delaware District Press Association, the Hubert H. Humphrey International Journalism Fellows, and the Alfred Friendly Press Fellows.

Callahan has been in journalism education since 1989, teaching graduate and undergraduate courses at Arizona State University, the University of Maryland at College Park, Columbia College of Chicago, and Boston University.

A New York native, Callahan and his wife, Jeanmarie, live in Scottsdale with their two sons Cody and Casey.

Leslie-Jean Thornton, a former reporter and editor, is an assistant professor at the Walter Cronkite School of Journalism and Mass Communication at Arizona State University. In her research and teaching, she specializes in online media, editing issues and journalism practice. She earned her doctorate at the University of North Carolina at Chapel Hill where she was a Freedom Forum Fellow. Before working on her Ph.D., she was an editor at newspapers in New York, Connecticut and Virginia, most recently at *The Virginian-Pilot* in Norfolk. In the early days of the Internet, an editor advised her to stop wasting her time teaching others in the newsroom how to use it. It's advice she's happily ignored ever since.

She is also a graduate of the journalism masters program at New York University and taught at the State University of New York at New Paltz, Mercy College, and Old Dominion University. Her husband, Randy Jessee, is a journalist and news systems expert.

CHAPTER 1

JOURNALISTS AND THE NET

I don't like computers. Never did really. I suspect I was the victim of bad timing. I was a journalism student in Boston in the late 1970s, just as computers were sweeping into newsrooms across the nation, but before they became commonplace in journalism classrooms. In my first job as a reporter in the wilds of northern New England, the computers crashed so often that they made me long for the days of banging out stories on the battered gray Royals back at the campus daily. But despite the early frustrations, writing on the computer—with the ability to quickly change words and sentences and move around chunks of a story—made our jobs easier, and our journalism products better.

Not long after my fledgling forays into the computer world, commercial databases began springing up, giving reporters the ability to quickly access background for stories on deadline. Systems such as Lexis-Nexis, though expensive, became important additions to the journalist's reporting arsenal, and the systems were fairly easy to use. They came with directories of files and standardized keyword search systems. Many reporters today could not imagine trying to background a story without an electronic database.

Today, the new frontier for computer-savvy journalists is the Internet.

—C. C.

WHAT IS THE INTERNET?

The Internet has seemingly come from nowhere to be omnipresent in our culture in the past decade. In fact, the Internet is more than 30 years old, a creation of the Defense Department. Unlike commercial databases such as Lexis-Nexis, there is no Internet Corp., no single institution called the Internet. Instead, the Internet is, at its essence, simply a network of attached computer networks. The Internet system allows users to go from one computer network to another. Users can quickly move from a college in New England to a library in Australia to a military installation in California. Users can be said to be "on" the Internet, but they are "in" the Australian library, New England college or California military base. This is a critically important distinction for journalists trying to evaluate the accuracy and value of the information they are finding.

Although it has been around for decades, the Internet was used mostly by the military and academia until fairly recently. Technological advancements in the early 1990s led to the creation of the World Wide Web, a graphically oriented part of the Internet that allows users to point and click on text, images, audio, and video. The intuitive point-and-shoot design of the Web was much easier to master than the earlier architectures of the Internet and led to extraordinary growth.

Estimating the size and usage of the Internet is difficult. Internet World Stats (www.internetworldstats.com), a company that specializes in international market research and Web usage statistics, reports there are more than 1.1 billion users online worldwide as of March 2007. That's up from an estimated 513.4 million users as of August 2001, a figure that represented a twenty-fold increase from six years earlier.

The Internet Software Consortium (www.isc.org) attempts to measure the growth of the Internet by estimating the number of Internet hosts—computers that are connected directly to the Internet—around the world. The consortium's January 2001 survey found 109.6 million computer hosts, a 100-fold increase in eight years. The chart (see Figure 1.1), based on ISC data, shows the staggering growth in computers connected directly to the Internet over 11 years. The rise in connections from 1981 to 1994 was omitted from the chart since the rise was barely perceptible visually. In 1981, there were 213 connections. In 1994, there were 3,212,000. But that pales compared to 439,286,364 connections in July 2006.

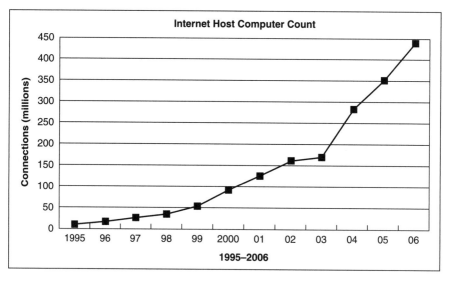

FIGURE 1.1   **Internet Host Computer Count**

WHY SHOULD JOURNALISTS CARE
ABOUT THE INTERNET?

Today the Internet stands as the single largest source of information available anywhere in the world. And from a reporter's perspective, the Net will only get better as more and more information is added. The possibilities for information-hungry journalists are limitless. It also is relatively inexpensive, as low as $10 or so a month for unlimited use. That stands in stark contrast to many of the bill-by-the-minute commercial databases that can run a newsroom tens of thousands of dollars a year. But there's a catch. Because of the way the Internet has grown up—in a piecemeal fashion without much design or forethought—there is no one single way to search comprehensively for information. That can leave the unprepared journalist frustrated, with nothing to show for his or her efforts other than hours wasted surfing around the Net, busted deadlines, and angry editors. And the incredible growth of the Web can add to a reporter's frustration, with sites coming and going daily and addresses constantly changing.

In the final analysis, is it worth the hassle? Yes, without question. Reporters around the country have developed stories that they would never have been able to do—or stories that would have been too costly or too time-intensive to go after—without the Internet. Throughout this book, we will hear from journalists who have used the Internet to track tornadoes in Minnesota, investigate the state of fisheries and wetlands, analyze standardized tests in elementary schools and detail how recycled hazardous waste gets into fertilizer. And that's not to mention the less sexy but just as important everyday uses that help save valuable time and add depth to breaking news stories.

Does that mean that if you are not an Internet expert you will never be a great journalist? Of course not. Some of the best journalists in the country don't know a Web site from a spider web, but continue to produce award-winning journalism. It does mean, however, that having the basic skills of Internet reporting will make your journalism better—in some cases through saved time that can be put into other aspects of a story, sometimes through more in-depth reporting, and in other cases through new stories not available elsewhere.

THINKING STRATEGICALLY ABOUT THE NET

In talking with journalists around the country, we find a large number who have given the Net a whirl, only to get frustrated with its idiosyncrasies and give up on it altogether. The problem is not the Net, but lack of a strategic plan to attack it. Many journalists and journalism students approach the Internet as they would a commercial database. That is to say, facing a

■ ■ ■ ■ ■ ▨▨▨▨▨▨▨▨▨▨▨▨▨▨▨▨▨▨▨▨▨▨▨▨▨▨▨▨▨▨▨▨▨▨

BOX 1.1

Duff Wilson, as an investigative reporter at the Seattle Times, *explains how he used the Internet to help show how toxic wastes were getting into farm fertilizer.*

At least 10 states and the federal government launched investigations into toxic wastes in fertilizer because of *Seattle Times* reports that would have been simply impossible without the Internet.

The Web was my worldwide medical librarian, agronomist, biologist, toxicologist, lawyer, regulator, and, of course, telephone operator and postal carrier. So it seemed. I used Web sites, newsgroups, and e-mail almost every day during and after publication.

"Fear in the Fields—How hazardous wastes become fertilizer" was an in-depth series of articles published starting July 3, 1997.

(www.seattletimes.nwsource.com/news/speicla/fear_fields.html)

The articles showed how some heavy industries save millions of dollars by disposing of hazardous wastes as fertilizer and other farm soil supplements.

All over the United States, farmers were unknowingly using this recycled waste—sometimes with calamitous results they couldn't understand. And this was all being done legally, in the name of recycling, with virtually no governmental oversight or regulation.

I learned about this problem from the whistle-blowing mayor of the small farm town of Quincy, Washington. Her opponents—the big farms and chemical companies—tried to shut her up by threatening to sue her for another Alar "scare." The Web helped me document the complaints carefully, though, and put Quincy in a national and global context.

Among the Internet tools that were most helpful:

- Industrial Material Exchange sites, quiet little corners of the Web where waste brokers sell or give away toxic materials. I compared them to blind-dating services.
- Medline, the free index to 9 million medical journal articles from around the world. Many of the non-English ones have English language summaries. This service from the National Library of Medicine gets my vote for the most helpful site on the Web. One of my best searches cross-matched *cadmium* and *fertilizer.*
- Experts of every stripe dug up from DejaNews, Liszt and Reference.com newsgroups and mailing lists.
- The Right-to-Know Network's database covering the Environmental Protection Agency's Toxic Release Inventory. I found official government reports on industries sending hazardous wastes to fertilizer manufacturers.

In addition, I used general search engines to find a wealth of information about heavy metals and dioxins and fertilizer. Yahoo is my favorite search engine because of its generosity in linking to other search engines.

Yahoo eventually led me to a Colorado company, CoZinCo, that was publishing chemical analyses of fertilizer products. They showed up to 5 percent lead contents, and, as I found out through other Web articles as well as interviews and tree-killing material (paperwork), the lead can be very dangerous indeed.

Since the articles were published, people from around the world have tuned in through our *Seattle Times* Web site. I also used the Internet to send out every article as it was published in this corner of the country to an informal mailing list of more than 50 people around the globe. This way, they could read the full versions, and I could immediately solicit their follow-up ideas and their all-important input on the fairness, accuracy, and completeness of each article.

---

deadline, they jump on the Net, punch in a few key words and begin "surfing" around. After a few tries—and failures—they get off-line as quickly as they jumped on. Let me recommend a more targeted, tiered approach that will cut down on frustration while improving results and boosting confidence.

Reliable Sites. Forget "surfing," at least at the beginning. The first foray into using the Internet in a deadline reporting setting should be simply to begin using sites that you know are going to lead to the sought-after information. Chapters 4, 5, and 6 detail more than 100 of the best Internet sites available for journalists today. Focusing on this method will build your confidence in both the Internet's ability to help your reporting and in your ability to use the Internet.

Think Past the Rolodex. The Internet provides reporters with the opportunity to get beyond their Rolodex list of usual sources, providing greater depth and breadth to their journalism. It is especially useful for tapping into state and federal government sources for information affecting the local community. Traditionally, community-based reporters have paid little attention to state and federal matters because of geographic constraints. But now, for instance, a reporter covering a single town can use the Internet to access detailed financial records on the area's biggest employers from the Securities and Exchange Commission, find out who locally is contributing to the upcoming congressional campaigns from a federal contributions database and get a jump on the Pentagon's plans for the local military installation from the Federal Register. We will look at this in more depth in Chapter 8.

Build an Electronic Beat System. Reporters should save and organize Internet sites they have discovered by "bookmarking" Web pages and organizing the bookmarks into files by topic area. Chapter 8 is devoted to conceptualizing an electronic beat system and how to create one for yourself.

■ ■ ■ ■ ■

BOX 1.2

The Internet played a critical role in a bankruptcy project headed by David Milliron when he was special projects editor at Gannett News Service. He is now at the Atlanta Journal-Constitution.

Despite a booming economy and the lowest unemployment rates in a generation, a record 1 million Americans headed into bankruptcy court in 1996 to fold their financial cards and ask for a new game. Gannett News Service wanted to know how the bankruptcy rate had grown, and where, down to the local level. The Internet was key to locating the necessary data for the project, which was published in March 1997. GNS revisited the issue of bankruptcies in February 1998.

The Internet led GNS to the American Bankruptcy Institute (ABI) in Alexandria, Virginia. The ABI publishes a multitude of bankruptcy statistics and analyses. A phone call to the ABI's data specialist pointed us to a data contact at the Administrative Office of the U.S. Courts, which told us the agency had a county-by-county database of aggregate bankruptcy data.

- Both personal and business filings, by type of filing, dating back to fiscal year 1991.
- The data, exclusively obtained for the first time by GNS, are kept in a popular word processing file format.

While awaiting delivery of the data, GNS continued gathering background for the package. Here are some of the useful Internet sites GNS used:

- The American Bankruptcy Institute site (at www.abiworld.org) contains a news section with bankruptcy news headlines from newspapers, press releases and other sources, plus a bankruptcy library section, and a section on legislative news.
- The U.S. Courts' Home Page (at www.uscourts.gov) provided information on the various types of bankruptcy filings, the number of bankruptcy judges, and contacts at the Administrative Office of the U.S. Courts.
- The Federal Reserve site (at www.federalreserve.gov.) contains "Domestic and International Research Statistics," which has links to current and historical data, including the monthly "G.19" consumer credit report.
- The National Bankruptcy Review Commission site (at www.nbrc. gov) provided background documents and testimony being gathered for its presidential report on the state of the bankruptcy system.

Think Institutionally. Once the top Web sites from Chapters 4, 5, and 6 have been incorporated into your reporter's toolbox, you will be ready to search for specific information. In commercial database searches, we use keyword searches. If we are researching a story on the growth of

■ ■ ■ ■ ■

BOX 1.3

Jo Craven was a member of the Washington Post *computer-assisted reporting team when she used the Internet in a variety of ways for a major investigation into the Unification Church. She later went to* Newsday *and* The New York Times.

Time was short: *Washington Post* reporters Marc Fisher and Jeff Leen were given less than a month to explore the operation of the Reverend Sun Myung Moon, a religious leader with a reputation for using a variety of businesses to gently weave his way into the fabric of a community. His motivation, church leaders and critics said, is to provide employment to his followers, to gain influence in industries he considers crucial for recognition of himself as Messiah and to support his spiritual and political agenda.

Because Moon's operation—dubbed Moon Inc. by Fisher and Leen—spans continents, the reporters decided to concentrate on the Washington metro area and the Internet provided a helpful jump-start to the project.

Researcher Alice Crites combed the Net for information on Moon and came up with a list of possible connections—businesses, including seafood companies, media groups, jewelers, dance troupes, and others with an estimated value of $300 million—that we suspected were owned or sponsored by Moon and his circle.

The next step was to prove the connection.

Using a dial-up bulletin board system (BBS) operated by the Virginia Corporation Commission, I checked the incorporation papers of more than 30 businesses and found the links we were looking for; while Moon and his known allies were rarely listed as owner or president of the companies, time and again, I found one or more of them listed in the next tier, as officers or directors.

As we unraveled Moon's connections to these companies, Fisher and Leen called on many of them, and, in a very short time, stitched together a comprehensive profile of Moon Inc.

We also used a variety of other Internet resources, with varying success: On the off-chance that some of the companies might be publicly held, Crites and I checked Securities and Exchange Commission records on the Internet; I used several on-line phone and E-mail directories to help Fisher locate some sources outside of the Washington area; and I used another BBS to search for lawsuits against Moon.

While all of the records we searched are available, often with more detail, on paper, accessing them electronically gave us what we needed and saved us a lot of time on a tight deadline.

women farmers and want statistics, we might type in keywords such as *women* and *farmers* into a commercial database. But such a search likely would produce poor results on the Internet because of its vastness. A better approach would be to think institutionally. What institution—association, organization, governmental agency, lobbying group, company—might have the information we are seeking? Instead of using *women* and *farmers* as the Internet keywords, we might instead look for "likely suspects," institutions that are likely to have the information. In this case, the Census Bureau and the U.S. Department of Agriculture might be logical places to search. Thinking institutionally in Internet searches can save valuable time. We will explore this strategy more in Chapter 7.

Search Engines as the Last Resort. Searching by institution only works if you have some idea what sites may have the information you are seeking. If you don't know, then you must plunge into the final frontier of the Internet for journalists: surfing for information with directories and search engines. This is the most used method by nonjournalists, but for deadline-conscious reporters, it should be the least frequently employed method. We will explore various searching strategies and specific search engines in Chapter 7.

Before we begin our journey into the world of journalistic uses of the Internet, we need to know a little bit about how to evaluate the information we find there.

CHAPTER 2

EVALUATING INFORMATION FROM THE INTERNET

MYTHS ABOUT THE INTERNET AND CREDIBILITY

There are a lot of misconceptions about the Internet, particularly when talking about the reliability of information found there. Some people—and novices fall into this category more than most—seem to place a credibility blanket over the Net. If it is on the Net, the thinking goes, it must be right.

Then there is the other extreme, folks—and some veteran editors and reporters seem to be in this camp—who have heard about the rumor-mongering and other bad information floating around in cyberspace and immediately dismiss everything on the Net as not credible.

The problem with both ways of thinking is that they conceptualize the Internet as a single entity. As we discussed in Chapter 1, the Internet is not an information source in itself; it is, rather, a conduit to get to various sources of information. Therefore, it does not matter whether the information was obtained via the Internet. What matters is where that information came from, the original source. Dismissing or accepting information simply because it was obtained from the Internet is the equivalent of rejecting or embracing information simply because it came from a newspaper, book, or magazine. In traditional reporting, we do not evaluate information based on its form; we evaluate it on the credibility of the source that is producing the information. Both *The New York Times* and the *National Enquirer* are newspapers, printed products that disseminate news in paper form. But we place different levels of credibility on information in those publications based on our knowledge of the products. That is the same analysis we must perform when evaluating information on the Internet.

WHAT'S OUT THERE?

While the analysis we perform to determine credibility is the same, whether the information comes in printed paper form or digitally, the Internet does make the job a bit more cumbersome for one reason: It is much cheaper to "publish" on the Internet than to publish a book, newspaper, magazine, or report. Therefore, there is a lot more junk on the Net. In fact, the overwhelming majority of what can be found on the Internet could never be used in a news story. Then why bother? Simple. The Internet is so vast, even if only a small fraction of the information available meets our journalistic litmus tests for credibility, that still represents an enormous amount of valuable information that otherwise might be difficult or expensive or time-consuming to obtain.

DECODING WEB ADDRESSES

To evaluate the credibility of Internet-gathered information, a reporter must determine the source of that information. And the key to determining the source of information is to decode the World Wide Web address. A basic Web address consists of a series of letters, which often form words, separated by periods, which in Internet parlance are referred to as *dots*. For instance, the main address for the White House is:

> www.whitehouse.gov

Let's deconstruct this address. The "www" stands for the World Wide Web. Most (but not all) Web sites begin with www. Next "whitehouse" is clearly descriptive of the Web site. Finally, we see the suffix "gov." That stands for government. Web addresses end in two- or three-letter codes that indicate, generally, what type of entity is publishing the Web site. When analyzing Web sites, immediately go to the suffix. Some common suffixes in the United States include:

> .gov = Governmental sites, usually federal
> .us = State and local governments
> .edu = Education, including colleges and universities
> .mil = U.S. military sites
> .org = Nonprofit organizations and associations
> .int = International organizations
> .com = Commercial
> .net = Networking organizations

Federal Government and Military Sites

Analyzing the suffixes goes a long way in helping to determine the source. Only official government entities are allowed to use the .gov suffix. Does that mean everything found on the Internet with the .gov suffix is reliable and credible? Of course not, just as every government official or every government document is not reliable and credible. What can be concluded is that information found on the Internet with a .gov address has come from an official government—usually federal—entity. And once the source has been determined, the Internet-accessed information from those entities can be treated in the same way as information received in paper form. The same is true of the .mil suffix. The .mil suffix shows that the Web site is run by a branch of the Defense Department and should be evaluated accordingly.

State and Local Government Sites

Most local government sites in the United States—state, county and city—publish with the .us suffix. They often—but not always—follow a standardized template. States are usually found at www.state.??.us, where the question marks represent the two-initial state abbreviation. Similarly, many counties and cities can be found at www.co.(name).??.us and www.ci.(name).??.us, where co and ci stand for city and county respectively and name is the full name or abbreviation of the county or city—omit the parentheses—followed by the state abbreviation and the .us ending.

Educational Institutions

The .edu site is not quite as clear-cut. Only educational institutions—colleges and universities—are given Web addresses with the .edu suffix. But those institutions often give their students the ability to publish on the Web. That's great for free speech and expression, but not so great for journalists who need to know whether the information is coming from Harvard University or the 18-year-old freshman sitting in his dorm room at 3 A.M. and sharing the meaning of life with the world. Needless to say, it is usually self-evident which site is from the student and which is from a bunch of academics and administrators (for one, the student site is almost always more creative). But reporters, who should have a healthy dose of skepticism about getting the cyber-wool pulled over their eyes, should make sure that what looks like the Harvard Law School site is not really a *Lampoon* spoof. Here is a simple way: College sites have addresses that refer to their subdivisions. For instance, the Web address for the University of Maryland's School of Architecture is:

> www.arch.umd.edu

Here, we see the main address for the university: "www" for the World Wide Web, "arch" is the university's abbreviation for Architecture, "umd" stands for the University of Maryland and "edu" is the suffix ensuring us that the Web site is from a bona fide institution of higher learning. Student sites usually have their name or some nickname in their address. Student John Smith's Maryland address, for instance, might look like this:

> www.wam.umd.edu/~jsmith/home.htm

The tilde (~) indicates that the organization has given an individual access to publish on its Web site, but that the person does not necessarily represent the home organization. For journalists, the tilde should be a giant red flag.

Another way to ensure the credibility of a university-based Internet site is to get on the institution's main page and point and click to the site that contains the information being evaluated. Colleges traditionally link only to their own Web pages, not to students' individual sites.

Nonprofit Organizations

Nonprofit organizations and associations pose a different problem for reporters. A Web address with the .org suffix indicates that the information is coming from a nonprofit organization, in much the same way the .gov suffix shows that the site is from a governmental body. And the same rules should apply. Say you received information from www.nra.org. This is the Internet site for the National Rifle Association. Should you conclude that all of the information you find on www.nra.org is 100 percent right (or 100 percent wrong)? No. You should determine simply that the information came from the NRA and weigh that information in the same fashion that you would analyze it if you received it in a more traditional form. The problem is, governmental agencies have a certain level of credibility and recognition. Reporters may, however, come across nonprofit organizations on the Internet that are unknown to them. The response in these cases should be the same as if the reporters were sent a press release or report from a group they never heard of: Check it out to determine the organization's credibility and whether it has particular biases. Who operates the group? Who is on its board? How long has it been in existence? Has it been used as an expert source of information by other press outlets?

International Sites

International organizations, such as the United Nations and NATO, carry the .int suffix. Individual country Web sites carry a two-initial suffix, an abbreviation of that country's name. For example, .au is Australia, .jp is Japan, and .ru is Russia.

Commercial Sites

The .com and .net suffixes denotes a commercial Web site. In other words, the .com or .net Web site found can be from absolutely anybody in the world who has paid the relatively small fee to get a registered Web address. Everyone from IBM to the kid down the block can have a .com or .net address. Needless to say, this is the most problematic area for reporters on the Internet. It would

FIGURE 2.1   The official White House site. (www.whitehouse.gov)

be easy—and safe—to simply ignore all .com sites, but that would eliminate some of the richest reportorial sites on the Web. Instead, treat the .com and .net sites the same as an .org address. If you know the company, say IBM, then evaluate the information as you would the same information in paper form from the company. If it is a commercial entity you never heard of, make sure you check it out.

The Web sites shown in Figures 2.1, 2.2 and 2.3 have similar addresses. Only the last part of the Web address is different. Figure 2.1, located at www.whitehouse.gov, is the official Internet site of the president of the United States. Figure 2.2, located at www.whitehouse.org, is a parody site that purports to offer official news and information but is a product of a company

FIGURE 2.2   A parody site. (www.whitehouse.org)

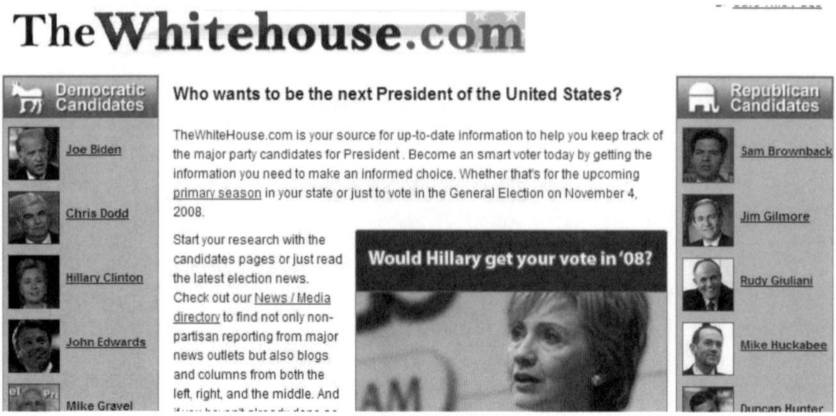

FIGURE 2.3   An information site. (www.whitehouse.com)

called Chickenhead. A previous (and quite famous) parody site was www.whitehouse.net, but at the most recent check, that no longer had the White House as its subject matter. Nor, for that matter, did another famous site that was located at www.whitehouse.com: between 1997 and 2004, it was a pornography site. In June 2007, it was a site dedicated to giving information on political candidates and linking to political news sources. Remember, always check the suffix first when trying to determine where you are.

New Web Addresses

The suffixes, like .info and .com, are known as generic top-level domains, or gTLDs. Thirteen new ones were added in 2000 and 2004, including .biz and .info, and another group is expected to be available in summer 2008. The Internet Assigned Names Authority at www.iana.org/gtld/gtld.htm can supply you with the latest information. Like .net and .com addresses, .biz, .info, and others are available commercially, and therefore should be treated from a journalistic perspective just like a .com address.

Third-Party Addresses

Many free services can take a long Web address (url) and redirect it to a shorter one, which can then be used in its place. Just cut and paste the multipart address into one of the sites' forms and it will be quickly assigned a new address. Caution: Spammers and others interested in masking their identities can use these services to hide affiliations that would be revealed in the longer addresses. Two of the most popular sites are Snipurl and Tinyurl. Both watch for inappropriate uses, such as spamming, and can deactivate an address if warranted.

TECHNIQUES FOR EVALUATING WEB SITE CREDIBILITY

Finding Web Page Owners and Operators

Addresses with .gov, .us, and .edu tell us definitely what organization is hosting a particular Web site. But as we have seen, the same is not true of the commercially available addresses (including .com, .net, .org, .info, .biz, and .travel). How can reporters be sure a .com or .org Web site is what it claims to be? We need to do a little investigating and check the official registration. A Web site registration check is a two-step process, but it isn't as easy as it used to be. As demand for addresses exploded, more registrars developed to handle them. The once-comprehensive "WhoIs" system splintered after deregulation. The good news, more sites offer the service. The bad news, they don't all work from the same database. Still, the first step involves going to a WhoIs site such as

http://whois.domaintools.com/

Type in the main address of the Web site you want to check and it will tell you which accredited registration service company the Web site is registered with. Then, go to that registration site and do a search there. Some sites will do both steps. See, for example,

www.betterwhois.com/

Truncating Web Addresses

Search engines (see Chapter 7) often will present matches that are deep inside a Web site. For instance, the biographical information at Arizona State University for Professor Tim McGuire is located at

http://cronkite.asu.edu/faculty/cv/mcguirecv.doc

By going directly to that address, it might not be clear what organization is sponsoring the site. To find out, simply cut off all of the information to the right of the first forward slash. That leaves just the main home page, which will indicate the sponsoring institution.

This method also is useful when a Web address produced by a search engine is no longer functioning. Web sites change often, and it could be that the information is still inside that Web site but on a different page. To find out, truncate the address and search on the main page for the item being sought.

Beware of Title Pages

A final warning involves the titles of Web pages. Look above the Location box and menu bar to the top of the browser software window and you will see a title. It can be helpful while reporting, but remember, it is simply a description written by the author of that page. One of the authors titled his personal home page with (cleverly) "Christopher Callahan," but he could have just as easily titled it "White House" or "The Boston Red Sox" or "King George," so be wary about page titles.

TRAVELING IN AND OUT OF WEB SITES

Hyperlinks can take you to one of three places on the Internet: to another place on the Web page you already have opened, to another page within the Web site, or to an entirely different Web site. For reporters, it is critical to always know where you are. Most Web sites have links to other sites, and if you are not paying close attention to the location box on top, you may think you are in the Web site you started in when in fact you are in an entirely different institution. This is not terribly important to the casual Internet surfer, but critical for reporters who need to evaluate the credibility of the information they are collecting. And just because one institution has links to an outside site does not mean that entity is giving its endorsement to the information in the linked site. For instance, the *Washington Post* provides its online readers with hyperlinks to area schools. That does not mean that the information in the schools' Web sites should be evaluated in the same way as the original content of the *Washington Post*.

Even traveling within the same site can be confusing. Think of a single Web site as an underground building. You first enter the ground floor on the home page and then travel deeper into the building. Each "floor" is separated by a forward slash. So when you click one flight down, the address in the Location box will look something like this:

www.university.edu/departments

Go down one more flight and it might look like this:

www.university.edu/departments/journalism

And still another flight down:

www.university.edu/departments/journalism/courses

The number of "floors" is limitless; therefore, in large Web sites, the addresses can get pretty complicated. Also, each "floor" can have separate pages, so the underground building begins to look more like an underground pyramid.

TRUTH OR SCARE?

You can pretty much figure out that an e-mail message asking you to deposit $25,000 in a bank and then send the details to a previously unheard of distant relative in another country isn't exactly on the level. But what if you come across an online news story from a reputable and respected source that reports Bill Gates has been arrested for breaking into NASA computers? The *Orange County Register*'s Web site was hacked in September 2000 and several sentences in a news story were changed to include that false information about Gates. In a story about the infiltration, *USA Today* reported that the story was online for about 45 minutes before the break-in was discovered and the correct story reposted.

A more recent Web error, known as the "51-second glitch," involved inadvertent publication of a "standby" headline (one of several written in advance in anticipation of breaking news) in washingtonpost.com. It reported that John Edwards had suspended his presidential campaign because of his wife's health. The story was, in fact, just the opposite. He had announced that he would *not* suspend his campaign. The correct story was up in under a minute, but that many seconds in Internet time might as well be forever when you consider how information is shared and archived. That same morning, a blog, Politico.com, carried the false Edwards report based on a single source who was wrong. CNN and MSNBC reported the Politico story online and on air and others followed suit.

The errors were quickly publicized and corrected, but the damage in such incidents can't be completely erased. How many e-mails forwarded those falsities? How often does seemingly accurate information get into other reporters' stories or distributed as news? How often does it get into search archives with no mention of the error? It's important to remember that misinformation is not always deliberate. As always, the point is that information has to be verified even if it seems perfectly valid. Here are some sites to help you do that, whether you're checking stories making the e-mail rounds or trying to assess the credibility of a Web site:

> *GoogleNews.* Because it's so quick to detect published stories, doing a keyword search on the story you're following can help you catch corrections and updates. Search on "correction," but don't consider that a comprehensive search.
> http://news.google.com

> *Snopes.* Rumors current and past. You can sign up for an RSS feed and e-mailed updates.
> www.snopes.com

> *McAfee.* Virus hoax listings.
> http://vil.mcafee.com/hoax.asp

> *FBI.* Internet fraud news. Offers news feeds and updates.
> www.fbi.gov/majcases/fraud/internetschemes.htm

NEWSROOM POLICIES
FOR INTERNET REPORTING

There are few written newsroom policies or guidelines about evaluating and attributing information found on the Internet, and the policies that do exist are often general. The Associated Press Guidelines for Responsible Use of Electronic Services is typical: "Apply the strictest standards of accuracy to anything you find on electronic services. The Internet is not an authority; authorities may use it, but so do quacks. . . . E-mail addresses and Web page sponsorship can easily be faked. Ask yourself, 'Could this be a hoax?' Do not publish . . . any electronic address without testing to see that it's a working address and satisfying yourself that it is genuine. Apply, in other words, your usual news judgment."

In fact, the "usual news judgment" recommended by the AP should be the mantra of journalists reporting out on the Internet. The form of the information received does not matter; what matters is the news value of the information and the legitimacy of the person or organization putting it out. If a group unknown in your newsroom comes out with a report, it does not matter whether that report was obtained via the fax, phone, mail, news conference, or Web site. The same process used to check out the organization should be employed.

And the information, if it is to be used in a news report, should be attributed in the same way. There should not be separate, new rules of attribution for information found on the Internet. If it is important to the story to mention how the news was obtained, and sometimes it is, then that should be included. But otherwise, routinely adding that the information was found on a company's Web site is the same as reporting that the information was transmitted to the reporter via a facsimile machine.

CHAPTER 3

HAVEN FOR RUMORS AND MISINFORMATION

The stunning growth of the Internet has provided journalists with unprecedented reporting opportunities. And unprecedented peril. In April 2001, the American Journalism Review *published "The Real Computer Virus," an in-depth look by* National Journal *White House correspondent Carl M. Cannon at the proliferation of rumors and misinformation on the Internet, and how those untruths often wind up in the mainstream media. The following is excerpted from Cannon's story (reprinted by permission of* American Journalism Review*).*

To commemorate independence last year, *Boston Globe* columnist Jeff Jacoby came up with an idea that seemed pretty straightforward. Just explain to his readers what happened to the brave men who signed the Declaration of Independence.

This column caused big trouble for Jacoby when it was discovered that he had lifted the idea and some of its language from a ubiquitous e-mail making the rounds. It touched a particular nerve at the *Globe,* which had recently forced two well-regarded columnists to resign for making up quotes and characters. Jacoby was suspended for four months without pay, generating a fair amount of controversy, much of it because he was the primary conservative voice at an identifiably liberal paper.

But there was a more fundamental issue at play than Jacoby's failure to attribute the information in the column: Much of what the e-mail contained was factually incorrect. To his credit, Jacoby recognized this flaw and tried, with some success, to correct it. Ann Landers, however, didn't. She got the same e-mail and simply ran it verbatim in her column.

Passing along what she described as a "perfect" Independence Day column sent to her from "Ellen" in New Jersey, Ann Landers' epistle began this way:

Have you ever wondered what happened to the 56 men who signed the Declaration of Independence?

Five signers were captured by the British as traitors and tortured before they died. Twelve had their homes ransacked and burned. Two lost their sons who served in the Revolutionary Army. . . . Nine of the 56 fought and died from wounds or hardships of the Revolutionary War. They pledged their lives, their fortunes and their sacred honor.

Landers' column—like Ellen's e-mail—goes on from that point to list names and explain the purported fates of many of the men. But this was not the "perfect" column Landers thought it was, for the simple reason that much of the information in it is simply false—as any Revolutionary War scholar would know readily.

I know because I interviewed some of them. R. J. Rockefeller, director of reference services at the Maryland State Archives, reveals that none of the signers was tortured to death by the British. E. Brooke Harlowe, a political scientist at the College of St. Catherine in St. Paul, Minnesota, reports that two of the 56 were wounded in battle, rather than nine being killed. Brown University historian Gordon S. Wood points out that although the e-mail claims that for signer Thomas McKean "poverty was his reward," McKean actually ended up being governor of Pennsylvania and lived in material comfort until age 83.

And so on. What Landers was passing along was a collection of myths and partial truths that had been circulating since at least 1995, and which has made its way into print in newspaper op-eds and letters-to-the-editor pages and onto the radio airwaves many times before. Mark Twain supposedly said, in a less technologically challenging time, that a lie can make it halfway 'round the world before the truth gets its boots on. The Internet gives untruth a head start it surely never needed. And what a head start: If an e-mailer sends a missive to 10 people and each person who receives it passes it on to 10 more, by the ninth transmission this message could reach a billion people.

This is the real computer virus: misinformation. Despite years of warnings, this malady keeps creeping its way into the newsprint and onto the airwaves of mainstream news outlets.

One of the things that makes the Internet so appealing is that anyone can pull things off of it. The other side of the coin is that anyone can put anything on it. This poses a particular challenge for reporters who are taught in journalism school to give more weight to the written word (get the official records!) than to something they hear—say, word-of-mouth at the corner barber shop. But the Web has both official documents and idle gossip, and reporters using it as a research tool—or even a tip sheet—do not always know the difference.

"Journalists should be really skeptical of everything they read online," says Sreenath Sreenivasan, a professor at the Columbia University Graduate School of Journalism. "They should be very aware of where they are on the Web, just the way they would be if they were on the street."

They aren't always.

In November 1998, *The New York Times* pulled off the Web—and published—a series of riotously funny Chinese translations of actual Hollywood hits. *The Crying Game* became "Oh No! My Girlfriend Has a Penis!" *My Best Friend's Wedding* became "Help! My Pretend Boyfriend Is Gay." *Batman and Robin* was "Come to My Cave and Wear This Rubber Codpiece, Cute Boy."

If those seemed, in the old newsroom phrase, too good to check, it's because they were. They came from an irreverent Web site called topfive.com, which bills itself as offering "dangerously original humor."

But even after the *Times* issued a red-faced correction, the "translations" kept showing up. On January 5, 1999, Peter Jennings read the spoof of the title of the movie *Babe* ("The Happy Dumpling-To-Be Who Talks and Solves Agricultural Problems") as if it were factual. Jennings issued a correction 13 days later for his *World News Tonight* gaffe, but that didn't stop things. On April 16, 1999, some of the bogus translations showed up on CNN's *Showbiz Today*. On June 10, a *Los Angeles Times* staff writer threw one of the top five .com titles into his sports column. In Hong Kong, he claimed, the title *Field of Dreams* was "Imaginary Dead Ballplayers in a Cornfield."

"What journalists need to do is learn to distinguish between the crap on the Web and the good stuff," says Yale University researcher and lecturer Fred Shapiro. "It's a crucial skill and one that some journalists need to be taught."

Some of the high-level research sites on the Web are not easily accessible outside a university setting. That is to say, they are not free, which is a problem at news organizations, many of which have simply given reporters access to Lexis-Nexis and gotten rid of their librarians. Shapiro, who is editing the forthcoming *Yale Dictionary of Quotations,* is one of the foremost practitioners of how to use high-end Internet sites such as JSTOR and others aimed at scholars.

While using JSTOR, Shapiro recently came across an interesting little discovery. The phrase "There's no such thing as a free lunch" did not originate with economist Milton Friedman (who wrote a 1975 book of that name), as Shapiro rival *Bartlett's Quotations* says. Using the JSTOR site, which stands for journal storage, Shapiro found that another economist, Alvin Hansen, was already using it in 1952. The good news is that Yale's Shapiro is scooping *Bartlett's.* The bad news is that Hansen was a Harvard man.

"That's the best of the Web," Shapiro says. "I can get stuff in a few seconds that would take me years of going through the stacks."

This is the true appeal of the Net to working journalists. Even the most harried academic has more time to peruse original documents or wander through private libraries than we do. Often we don't even have hours. Speed is our métier. Yet any reporting worth pursuing requires drinking deeply at the well of historical context. The Internet gives us the chance to have our cake and eat it, too.

Even before President Clinton stirred up controversy with a slew of late-term pardons and commutations, I researched and wrote a 4,000-word article on the historical and legal underpinnings of a U.S. president's power to grant pardons, commutations, and clemency orders. One pertinent constitutional question was whether there are any real restrictions on the presidential pardon authority.

Logging onto Lexis-Nexis, I found several relevant, in-depth law review articles. Some of them cited Internet links to the original cases being cited. In fact these were highlighted "hyperlinks," meaning that with a single click of my mouse I was able to read the controlling Supreme Court cases dating back to Reconstruction. Within seconds of clicking on those Supreme Court links, I was gazing at the actual words of Salmon P. Chase, the chief justice appointed by Abraham Lincoln. Justice Chase answered my question rather unequivocally: "To the executive alone is entrusted the power of pardon," he wrote with simple eloquence, "and it is granted without limit."

This is not an isolated example. I cover the White House for *National Journal* and, like many of my colleagues, I have developed an utter reliance on the Internet. I do research and interviews on-line, find phone numbers, check facts and spellings and research the clips. I can read court cases on-line, check presidential transcripts, find the true source of quotes and delve into history.

Some days this is a tool that feels like a magic wand. The riches of the Web are as vast as the journalist's imagination.

During the NATO bombardment of Serbia, I wrote a piece examining the way governments use language during wartime. Years earlier, University of Virginia scholar William Lee Miller had quoted George Orwell to me on this very point. I wanted that quote, but Miller couldn't put his hands on it again, and I couldn't locate it on Lexis-Nexis. I figured I might find it on the Web, and I wasn't disappointed. I logged on to one of the several Orwell Web sites I found through my Yahoo! search engine. One of them had put up Orwell's actual newspaper columns from World War II–era Britain. I found just what I was looking for; it became my lead.

Last summer, while doing research for a lengthy opus about capital punishment in America, my interest was piqued in the great Leopold–Loeb murder trial, the first "Trial of the Century." Logging onto the Net, I was able to find several cogent synopses of that trial, as well as excerpts from Clarence Darrow's legendary 12-hour summation in which he pleaded for the court to spare the youthful killers from the gallows. I used his quotes—and the quotes of the Chicago prosecutor—in my piece.

The point of these examples is that the Internet has rapidly become such a valuable research tool that it's hard to remember how we did our jobs without it. Need that killer Shakespeare reference to truth-telling from *As You Like It* to spice up that Clinton legacy piece? Log on and find it. Fact-checking the Bible verses slung around by the candidates during the 2000 presidential election? The Bible is not only on the Web but is searchable with a couple of keystrokes. Attorney General John Ashcroft's Senate voting record is there, too, along with his controversial interview with *Southern Partisan* magazine.

Yet in recent months I have found myself quietly checking the validity of almost everything I find in cyberspace and whenever possible doing it the old-fashioned way: consulting reference books in libraries, calling professors or original sources on the phone, double-checking everything. I don't trust the information on the Net very much anymore. It turns out the same technology that gives reporters access to the intellectual richness of the ages also makes misinformation ubiquitous. It shouldn't come as a surprise, but a tool this powerful must be handled with care.

These problems are only going to get worse unless Net users—and journalists—get a whole lot more careful. According to the Nielsen//NetRatings released on February 15, 2001, 168 million Americans logged onto the Web in the first month of the new millennium.

Seven years ago, AJR warned that an over-reliance on Lexis-Nexis was leading to a "misinformation explosion." Since that time, the number of journalists using the data retrieval service has increased exponentially; at many news organizations, libraries have been phased out and reporters do their own searches. This has led, predictably, to an entire subgenre of phony quotes and statistics that won't die.

Ten years ago in an Associated Press story out of Mexico City, an opposition leader named Vicente Fox was identified as "the Harvard-educated Fox, a former president of Coca-Cola Co. in Mexico," information that apparently came in campaign-trail boasts Fox made himself. When he burst onto the international scene recently, the Harvard angle was repeated in hundreds of news outlets around the world. The *Chicago Tribune, USA Today,* the *Arizona Republic* and the *Fort Worth Star-Telegram* all referred to Fox as a Harvard man. *Business Week* used the curious phrase "executive diploma from Harvard Business School," and the *Boston Globe,* which you'd think could check with Harvard pretty easily, said Fox "spent a year studying at Harvard."

The problem, as *Forbes* magazine discovered, was that Harvard has no record of Fox ever studying there. Forbes found what seems to be the connection: In 1968, Coca-Cola brought in several Harvard Business School professors for six weeks of seminars with some of its best executives—including a young comer named Vicente Fox.

Former President Clinton, in one of his stock speech lines, often quotes Alexis de Tocqueville as saying, "America is great because America is good." It's a line that has been used by Presidents Dwight D. Eisenhower and Ronald Reagan and numerous presidential wannabes, including Patrick J. Buchanan and Phil Gramm. It's a nice sentiment, but de Tocqueville didn't say it.

This fact was unearthed by Claremont McKenna College professor John J. Pitney, who stumbled across the fake quote after assigning students in his class to find an example of a politician's use of a de Tocqueville saying and then write about whether it was used accurately and in context. One student took Clinton's quote and then went line by line through de Tocqueville's *Democracy in America*. Only trouble was, neither the quote, nor anything like it, is there at all.

After some sleuthing, Pitney discovered that the passage comes from an otherwise forgettable 1941 book about religion and the American dream. Pitney wrote about this, but Clinton and his speechwriters kept using the quote anyway. After all, it was in the database.

Sometimes the proliferation of such errors carries more serious implications. A couple of years ago, Diane Sawyer concluded a *PrimeTime Live* interview with Ellen DeGeneres the night her lesbian television character "came out" by reciting what Sawyer called "a government statistic": gay teenagers are "three times as likely to attempt suicide" as straight teenagers.

This factoid, which Sawyer said was provided to her by DeGeneres, is a crock.

Sleuthing by a diligent reporter named Delia M. Rios of Newhouse News Service revealed that this figure is not a government statistic, but rather the opinion of a single San Francisco social worker. In fact, a high-level interagency panel made up of physicians and researchers from the U.S. Department of Health and Human Services, the Centers for Disease Control, the National Institute of Mental Health and other organizations concluded that there is no evidence that "sexual orientation and suicidality are linked in some direct or indirect manner."

Yet, the bogus stat is still routinely cited by certain gay-rights activists, and thanks to Internet-assisted databases, has made its way into the *New York Times,* the *Chicago Tribune,* the *Los Angeles Times*—and onto prime time network television.

Massachusetts Governor William F. Weld cited the three-times-more-likely statistic while announcing that he was appointing a high-level commission to study gay and lesbian youth. But facts matter. Weld's commission was a public relations victory in the minds of some gay-rights activists, but others feared that basing the formation of such a task force on a phony statistic about suicide may represent a step backward for the actual well-being of gay youths. For starters, it creates an image of gay teens as emotionally vulnerable and uncertain, a stereotype that plays into the assertions from cultural conservatives who portray gay people in general as unhappy and misguided.

Joyce Hunter, one-time president of the National Lesbian and Gay Health Association, insists that the available evidence suggests that both gay and straight teens are, instead, emotionally resilient people who "go on to develop a positive sense of self and who go on with their lives." Other clinicians fear that this misinformation could turn into a self-fulfilling prophecy. Peter Muehrer of the National Institutes of Health says he worries that a public hysteria over gay-teen suicide could contribute to "suicide contagion," in which troubled gay teens come to see suicide as a practical, almost normal, way out of their identity struggles.

Another strain of the misinformation virus is spread by e-mail. The Internet has proven irresistible to a shadowy class of pranksters, ideologues, and gossips who routinely forward messages that tend to confirm their fears or prejudices—no matter how outlandish they are on their face.

One e-mail message that has ricocheted around the world a few times purports to be a warning from a police department in some city or other—Dallas was one of them—about the unsuspecting moviegoer who sat down in a theater only to be pricked by needles. Beside the needles is a written sign saying something like, "You have been infected with HIV. Welcome to the world of AIDS."

Another e-mail that received wide circulation claimed that a new scientific study had established a causal link between the use of underarm antiperspirants and breast cancer. A third tells a harrowing story of the traveling businessman (in some versions it's a woman in a bar) who is drugged and later awakens in a strange hotel room, hooked up to an intravenous needle—and minus one kidney.

These stories, all of which are patently untrue, are urban legends, pure and simple, but when they come over the computer, even educated people sometimes have given them credence. Everyone knows that the Net has no gatekeepers, and that this is its charm as well as its pitfall, but the written word tends to convey more authority than the spoken word. And this is the written word in real time.

"If there is something insidious, it's that there seems to be a surprising degree of credibility given to things that come through e-mail," U.S. Postal Service spokesman Norm Scherstrom told Mark Johnson, a reporter who debunked some of these cybermyths for Media General newspapers. "E-mail seems somehow urgent—it must be very cutting edge because it came electronically."

It's easy to make light of such stories, and democracy can probably thrive despite the existence of gullible geeks who check their movie seats for needles or who think their lives depend on not wearing underarm spray or even the fools who nervously check their abdomen every once in a while for that telltale scar that would confirm they'd been kidnapped the night before. But misinformation can carry a frightful price.

Late last year, South African President Thabo Mbeki was surfing the Net one night when he came across a quirky but authoritative-sounding Web site dedicated to the proposition that the HIV virus does not cause AIDS. This theory has been around as long as AIDS has been known, and it has been thoroughly discredited. Mbeki presides over a country where AIDS poses a human disaster of biblical proportions, and where the euphoria over shedding apartheid has been muted by an invisible killer that is decimating his people.

Perhaps then it is no wonder that, desperate, Mbeki would reach for a silver bullet. But in doing so he probably has assisted many South Africans to an early grave. He has ignored price discounts offered by pharmaceutical companies for life-saving drugs such as AZT, refused to aggressively have his government set up distribution networks for condoms, stacked an advisory panel with scientists who question whether AIDS is always fatal, and spoken publicly about the disease in ways that have confounded health-care workers in his country and sown confusion among South Africans.

Junk science on the Web—or junk history—has a way of oozing into the mainstream media, often because it proves irresistible to disc jockeys and radio talk-show hosts. The same is true of conspiracy theories and faulty understanding of the law, particularly when the incendiary subject of race relations is involved.

An e-mail marked "URGENT! URGENT! URGENT!" flew like the wind through the African American community for more than two years. It warned that blacks' "right to vote" will expire in 2007. The impetus for the e-mail was the impending expiration of the Voting Rights Act, which has since been renewed and, in any event, no longer has anything to do with guaranteeing anyone the right to vote.

Nonetheless, the preposterous claim was reiterated by callers to African American radio talk shows. Eventually, it prompted an official rebuttal by the Justice Department and a public disavowal by the Congressional Black Caucus. "The Web has good, useful information," observes David Bositis, senior political analyst for the Joint Center for Political and Economic Studies. "But it also has a lot of garbage."

This particular cyberrumor was eventually traced to a naive but well-intentioned college student from Chicago, who toured the South on a promotional trip sponsored by the NAACP. The mistaken notion that blacks' right to vote depends on the whims of Congress was given wide circulation in a guest column in *USA Today* by Camille O. Cosby, wife of entertainer Bill Cosby.

"Congress once again will decide whether African Americans will be allowed to vote," she wrote, echoing the e-mail. "No other Americans are subjected to this oppressive nonsense."

Black leaders went to great lengths to dispel this hoax, but it energized black voters. The ensuing higher-than-normal black turnout in the 1998 midterm elections helped Democrats at the polls, led to House Speaker Newt Gingrich's demise, and may have saved Bill Clinton's job. Could the e-mail hoax have played a role?

Other hoaxes are not so accidental. Last year, as the presidential campaign began heating up, I received an e-mail from a fellow journalist alerting me to an anti–Al Gore Web site she thought contained valuable information. It included a litany of silly statements attributed to Gore. Some of them were accurate, but several of them I recognized as being utterances of former Vice

President Dan Quayle. Others were statements never said by either Gore or Quayle.

On October 3, 1999, when liberal movie star Warren Beatty spoke to Americans for Democratic Action about his political views, he said that he wasn't the only one who worried that corporations were a threat to democracy. Beatty said that Abraham Lincoln himself had warned that corporations are "more despotic than monarchy," adding that Lincoln also said "the money power preys upon the nation in times of peace, and it conspires against it in times of adversity."

Beatty's populist version of Lincoln hardly squares with his career as a corporate attorney—he represented Illinois Central Railroad before he ran for public office—but that didn't faze modern journalists. "That Lincoln stuff just amazed me," gushed *Newsweek*'s Jonathan Alter on "Rivera Live." Alter wrote that Beatty's "harshest attacks . . . were actually quotes from a speech by Abraham Lincoln."

Actually, they weren't. Lincoln's official biographer once called the quote "a bold, unblushing forgery." And in a piece for History News Service, an on-line site that often debunks faulty history, Lincoln scholar Matthew Pinsker said this particular fake Lincoln citation has been around since 1896. In his speech at the 1992 Republican National Convention, Ronald Reagan attributed phony conservative sentiments to Honest Abe, including, "You cannot help the weak by punishing the strong," and "You cannot help the poor by destroying the rich."

This example underscores a couple of important caveats about the Web. First, bogus quotes were around a long time before the Internet. Moreover, the Net itself is often a useful tool for those trying to correct canards. Such was the case in a recent Internet hoax, this one targeting George W. Bush.

The extremely close election between Bush and Gore generated a blizzard of Web traffic, most of it in the form of assorted e-mails making fun of one political party or the other, or one candidate or the other—or Florida voters in general. But one outlandish anti-Bush e-mail pushed by disgruntled Democrats actually crept into numerous mainstream media outlets. This was the one in which 16th-century French monk Nostradamus predicted the outcome of this year's election—throwing in a partisan and gratuitous insult to boot: "Come the millennium, month 12, in the home of the greatest power, the village idiot will come forth to be acclaimed the leader."

This was so obviously fake—it doesn't sound remotely like Nostradamus—that it's hard to imagine anyone falling for it, let alone putting it in the newspaper. And yet it ran without comment at the end of a column in the *Times* of London, as unchallenged letters to the editor and reader comments in outlets ranging from California's *Ventura County Star* to Wilmington, North Carolina's *Morning Star*. Columnists at North Carolina's *Asheville Citizen-Times* and the *Tampa Tribune,* among other places, quoted it with little or no filter.

Meanwhile, a respected clearinghouse of information about Nostradamus issued a notice that the Bush e-mail was a hoax. It was, of course, a Web site.

In November 2001, the American Journalism Review *published an article by one of this book's authors that looked at one of these rumors and tried to show how such tales get started, and how they can spread so quickly, with such believability.*

BOX 3.1

By Christopher Callahan

Reprinted by permission of *American Journalism Review*

The night after the Sept. 11 attack, a sociology graduate student from Brazil named Marcio A. V. Carvalho tapped out an e-mail and sent it to an obscure Internet mailing list. The 488-word missive, which implied that U.S. policy brought on the terrorist strike, led with a startling accusation: That CNN video of Palestinians celebrating the attack was really Gulf War–era file footage from a decade earlier.

Carvalho's note, riddled with spelling and syntax errors and peppered with exclamation points and capitalizations for emphasis, offered no proof, saying only that the grad student had heard the claim from a professor, whom he did not name.

The story, as it turns out, was untrue. The video that aired on CNN and other networks was shot by a Reuters TV crew in the hours after the attacks on the World Trade Center and Pentagon. Yet with no further corroboration or elaboration from others, Carvalho's e-mail dispatch raced around the world at a speed only the Internet can provide. Within 24 hours, the story had spread so widely that the *St. Petersburg Times* included it in a piece trying to sort out Sept. 11 fact from fiction.

And despite a speedy retraction from Carvalho, denials from CNN and Reuters and no offers of proof from others, the story continued to spiral outward to the point where even CNN officials believe it could go down as a classic urban legend, as immortal as it is inaccurate.

The proliferation of rumors, gossip and urban legends in the Internet age is well documented. But how do such stories spread so quickly with such flimsy factual basis? Chris Cramer, president of CNN International Networks, believes "cyber-terrorism" is the culprit. "This was a concerted attempt to distort the news," Cramer says. Experts on Internet rumors, however, say how stories such as the Palestinian celebration video enter the public arena so quickly and with such force and credibility is a much subtler, more complex and less organized process than Cramer's "cyber-terrorism" label might imply.

The chain of events that rocketed the CNN rumor around the world started at 9:07 P.M. on Sept. 12 when Carvalho hit the send button and dispatched his note to the Social Theory Network, a seldom-frequented British-based electronic mailing list with 567 subscribers worldwide who share an interest in "the relationship between psychological and sociological explanations of the human condition."

In the message titled "Fourth Power," Carvalho said one of his professors claimed to have videotapes from 1991 "with the very same images" as the tape that aired on CNN. He urged his social theory colleagues to try to find a copy of the 1991 tapes, and said he would do the same. While Carvalho stated as fact "THOSE IMAGES WERE SHOT BACK IN 1991!!!," he never claimed to have the tapes or any proof of their existence.

Less than 31 hours later, an apologetic Carvalho posted a second note saying he had talked to the professor and she told him she was convinced she had seen the images 10 years earlier, but that she did not have any tapes. "I firmly believed that source, which proved to be untrustworthy," Carvalho wrote in a later e-mail to the list.

The genesis of rumors often comes from misunderstandings as opposed to organized attacks by so-called "cyber-terrorists," folklore experts say.

"Some might start as malicious attempts to undermine corporations, (but) most begin as innocent misunderstandings that escalate, snowball literally, because people think they might be true," says Mike Coggeshall, a cultural anthropologist and folklorist at Clemson University who studies urban legends.

And once the rumor that resonates with the public is loose on the Internet, it's nearly impossible to stop.

Carvalho's "Fourth Power" missive got little reaction from the Social Theory Network. Two members sent short reactions. But within hours, the note had escaped the relative isolation of the Social Theory Network as it began to be forwarded to friends and colleagues and posted on Internet news groups around the world.

Within six hours, it was posted on Independent Media Center, a Web site created by activists in the wake of the Seattle world trade protests. The center describes its mission as "the creation of radical, accurate and passionate tellings of the truth." That Web posting triggered an avalanche of e-mails and news group postings under headings such as "Media Manipulation," "Palestinians Images a Hoax," "Media Lies About Celebrating Palestinians," and "Sick and Tired of CNN's Lies and Manipulations."

But a review of dozens of these early messages show that they were little more than e-mailers adding their own opinions on top of Carvalho's forwarded message. So why did so many people believe it to be true? Scholars say the answer lies in the basic foundations for all folklore, no matter the medium.

"The reason (urban legends) spread and the reason they are semi believed is that they capture something in the mood of the people," says Clemson's Coggeshall. "They capture the hopes and concerns and fears."

David Emery, who runs the San Francisco–based Urban Legends and Folklore Web site at about.com, says this was the case with the CNN video rumor.

"You have to look at who most of the people who are passing it around are," he says. "And they are not people who have something against CNN. They are people who trust CNN and are suddenly gripped by the (notion) that maybe they can't."

The Internet, however, has changed the dynamics of folklore and the spread of urban legends.

Emery says the medium of e-mail makes it easier for people to pass along uncorroborated information. "It takes some effort and some sense of responsibility to spread a rumor by word of mouth. You actually have to call somebody or go next door," Emery says. People who would hesitate to pass along such information verbally often don't think twice about forwarding e-mail, he says.

Specialists in the world of folklore on the Internet also believe that e-mail dispatches carry more weight than verbal communications. "People are much more willing to grant credibility to anything that's written down," says Emery. "There is just something inherently more powerful in the written word than the spoken word."

Sreenath Sreenivasan, an associate professor of journalism at Columbia University who specializes in Internet communication, recalls the child's game "telephone," where a message gets passed from one person to the next, often with changes that by the end make the final iteration unrecognizable. "In e-mail, you see the exact thread in front of you. All the facts are there. You can't misreport it," he says. "Something I hear can be misreported."

But Sreenivasan believes the power of e-mail rumors goes beyond the simple fact that they are transmitted in text form. He says e-mail recipients often weigh the credibility of the sender, who typically is known to the recipient, as opposed to the original, usually unknown, author. "Your friend has sent you . . . an e-mail," Sreenivasan says. "In a way, I'm (thinking), 'I trust this guy, and he wouldn't just send me crap. He's serious, he's likeable.' I have a (credibility) rating in my mind for him, and he's acceptable."

And of course, there is the speed that comes with a mass delivery system such as e-mail.

"If I have a hot, juicy story, how many people can I call?" Sreenivasan asks. "It's really a problem to spread anything (verbally)." But with the Internet, he says, "in seconds I can tell 20 people or 100 people, and they can tell 20 people."

The CNN story reached critical mass less than 24 hours after the original dispatch—lightning speed even by today's digital standards. Reporters from around the world began calling CNN to confirm the Internet rumor the day after Carvalho's original posting, says Nigel Pritchard, vice president for public relations at CNN International Networks.

"It is extremely frustrating when you are trying to do the job of a news organization" and have to spend time knocking down a rumor "that is quite preposterous and obviously not true," Pritchard says.

Jim Romenesko says e-mails on the CNN rumor were "coming in fast and furious" to him at Media News, the popular Web site he runs in conjunction with the Poynter Institute. Romenesko says he received so many e-mails by the following day that he felt obliged to post one of the inquiries in the hopes of getting a response from CNN. Romenesko posted a brief inquiry from *Miami Herald* humor columnist Dave Barry—who said he "assumed this charge is nonsense" but was wondering if CNN had officially responded—and linked it to Carvalho's e-mail posted on the Independent Media Center.

The response came swiftly from Eason Jordan, the network's chief news executive. Jordan posted an e-mail in which he explained the video was shot in East Jerusalem by a Reuters crew on Sept. 11 "and included comments from a Palestinian praising Osama Bin Laden, who was not a Gulf War player."

But to try to kill a rumor once it has reached a mass audience is a near impossible task, and this one was no different. The proliferation of e-mails continued, as did calls to CNN.

Even Emery, whose Web site is devoted to debunking rumors and clarifying facts, says little can be done.

"I have no illusions that we stop the rumor or even slow rumors down very much, but you just try to get another viewpoint out there and get some facts out there to balance it so that people who do care (receive the) truth," Emery says. "It's just a fact that a lot of people don't really care. If it's a good (rumor), or meaningful to them emotionally, they simply pass it along."

The CNN rumor took a new turn on Sept. 18, six days after the Carvalho posting. An e-mail began circulating under the name of Russell Grossman, a spokesman for the BBC in London. A new flurry of e-mails traversed the Internet with what was described as confirmation from an "official source" — Grossman. The Islamic News and Information Network sent to its mailing list the new e-mail, noting that the network "is very careful to ensure that our reports come from reliable sources."

But even a cursory glance at the alleged smoking gun shows that it was not written by Grossman, but rather was a truncated version of Carvalho's original note with a single edit: Carvalho's "A teacher of mine, here in Brazil, has videotapes recorded in 1991" was replaced with "At the BBC here, we have these footages on videotapes recorded in 1991."

"The e-mail which is circulating wasn't sent by me or BBC Internal Communication and was not issued by the BBC," Grossman wrote in an e-mail to AJR. "It seems to be the work of someone seeking to make mischief." Cyber-terrorists may not have started the rumor or even aided significantly in its speedy promulgation around the world, but it seems they had a hand in keeping the story afloat.

Two days later, CNN posted an official denial, along with a similar statement from Reuters and a statement from Carvalho's school, Universidad Estala de Campinas–Brasil. The CNN statement urged readers to copy it and "send it to anyone you know who may have false information." But Internet folklorists say such corrections of popular rumors rarely get the same dissemination as the original story.

Indeed, both CNN and Romenesko continue to get calls and e-mail queries about the rumor. News organizations such as the *Atlanta Journal and Constitution, Milwaukee Journal Sentinel,* and *Columbus Dispatch* ran stories days after the Carvalho retraction and CNN denials to answer readers' continued inquiries about the rumor and try to set the record straight.

At press time, CNN's Pritchard told AJR he was receiving calls from Greek reporters saying they had received a press release allegedly confirming that the CNN video was from 1991. "I was told (there) was a press release," he says, but "nobody was able to show me."

"It spreads very quickly," a frustrated Pritchard says of the Internet rumors. "Like a wildfire."

CHAPTER 4

BASIC REPORTING RESOURCES AND REFERENCES

People seem to be having an awful lot of fun on the Internet. Even those who are not online can read print stories about people spending count-less hours listening to their favorite bands, learning about quirky hobbies or special interests that delight the mind and warm the heart, shopping 'til their fingers drop, connecting with old friends via e-mail and finding new ones in warm and fuzzy chat rooms where people sign off with smiley faces ☺!

This chapter is about none of the above. What we are going to explore is how serious journalists and journalism students can employ the Internet to better use some of the most basic reporting resources and reference tools for reporters and editors. In all of these cases, using these tools via the Internet is cheaper, faster, easier or a combination of all three.

TELEPHONE DIRECTORIES

The phone book and directory assistance are the most basic of newsroom resources, but they have their limitations, namely geographic. If you do not know the city or town of the person you are trying to track down, direc-tory assistance is of no assistance at all. And if you cannot identify a county or metropolitan area, the phone book is equally useless. But electronic tele-phone directories on the Internet provide the power of computing. Instead of searching through one county phone book at a time looking for the home phone number of a source, Internet phone directories allow you to search any geographic region, even the entire country, at the same time. Some good directories include:

> *Switchboard*   www.switchboard.com/
> *Yahoo People Search*   http://people.yahoo.com/
> *White Pages*   www.whitepages.com/
> *Argali White and Yellow (can download to desktop)*   www.argali.com/

Here is how they work, using Switchboard as the example. Say you are trying to track down this guy named Christopher Callahan. You know he lives in the northern part of Virginia, but do not have a street address, town or even a county. Type in the switchboard address and input as much information as you have (you need at least a last name). The ease of finding names is dependent in part on the unusualness of the person's last name. If all you have to find your source is the last name *Smith*, forget it. But in our example here, you have the first and last name and the region. Our first attempt at "Christopher Callahan" in Virginia turns up no results. But remember, a person may not be listed by his or her full first name. When we try "Chris Callahan," we get six "hits" back. We can quickly eliminate "Christina" and "Christine" because we know we are looking for a Christopher. Of the other four, only one — "Christoph A Callahan" — is in northern Virginia, and that turns out to be the one you are seeking.

Remember that the computer is dumb; it is only going to find what is out there, precisely as the information is listed. Because the phone book lists the name as Christoph instead of Christopher (guess the name is too long for the phone company), you would never have found him unless you entered an abbreviated form. Sometimes it may be necessary to use only an initial or perhaps just the last name. And if it is an unlisted number, that means it is unlisted on the Internet, too. These electronic directories also can be used to find businesses under yellow page sections and e-mail addresses.

Another type of directory search uses the phone number to find the person and address. This could be useful when trying to verify a phone number or check numbers called by a public official. A good phone number reverse directory is maintained by AT&T at www.anywho.com/rl.html.

MAPS

Like phone books, street maps are among the most basic of reporting tools. Squinting over the tiny print of a map in a darkened car is a not-so-glamorous, but oft-repeated behavior, as reporters race to the scene of a fire or try to find an obscure meeting place. Driving and reading a map at the same time are useful—albeit dangerous—art forms. Internet mapping programs, however, allow you to type in a specific address and get an instant print-out of the area. They also allow you to "zoom in" and "zoom out" on the area in question. Reporters about to leave for a story can reduce the inevitable getting-lost time by printing out two maps: a wide view that shows the location along with the nearest familiar thoroughfare and a close-up that shows every side street and cul-de-sac and even maps out where on a block the address is located.

Recent additions to mapping technology let you see the area in zoomable aerial views—sometimes even street-level views—and other options allow the overlay of real-time traffic conditions. Among the best mapping programs are:

MapQuest www.mapquest.com
Google Maps http://maps.google.com/maps
Yahoo! Maps http://maps.yahoo.com
Live Search (formerly MapBlast) http://maps.live.com/

The map in Figure 4.1, from Yahoo, shows driving conditions one afternoon in the area near Phoenix's Sky Harbor airport. Pop-ups give detailed information and color-coded dots and alert icons let you know the problem's severity. Good thing to check before heading out for a meeting or interview. Or to catch a flight.

In the Neighborhood? A Note about Accuracy

Before you plug in an address, zoom down in the aerial view as close as you can get and hit print, thinking you know exactly which building you're going to, think again. Chances are the map got you close, but a quick test suggests you at least check the house number once you get there.

We did a test run on a home and address we knew. The first map, on MapQuest, pinpointed a house that was two houses away (but the grab and

FIGURE 4.1 A Yahoo! Maps search from maps.yahoo.com

(Reprinted with permission of NavTeq. All rights reserved.)

pan animation was cool, as were the street labels in aerial view). Yahoo's aerial was nowhere near as good and it, too, got it *almost* right. GoogleMaps? Also wrong with yet another house in the same neighborhood. MSN Virtual Earth's Live Search nailed it. And if you wanted to know where the nearest gas station would be, you could check that, too.

Google's Street View launched in June 2007 with 360-degree panoramas available for San Francisco Bay, New York, Las Vegas, Denver and Miami. It's searchable by street address; Figure 4.2 focuses on a popular parking street near New York University's Journalism School. For a video tutorial on how to use Street View, click to http://youtube.com/watch?v=91wuBqlny50.

Map Mashups

Take two or more applications and mash them together and you've got a mashup that creates a new interactive information site—maps and traffic conditions, for example (see Figure 4.1). A site called HousingMaps merges Google maps and craigslist real estate listings (www.housingmaps.com). They are increasingly easy to create, which makes them not only a great reporting resource but an opportunity, in today's multimedia publishing world, to show and tell while involving the user. A few more examples include the Gawker Celebrity Stalker map (http://gawker.com/stalker), FindByClick .com, where you can locate bookstores and coffee shops, and Missing Kids Map (www.missingkidsmap.com).

GoogleMapsMania (http://googlemapsmania.blogspot.com) blogs the latest developments. Google has tutorials that keep getting easier. Go to

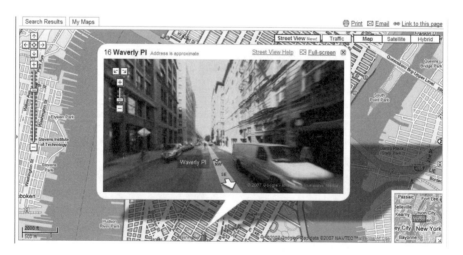

FIGURE 4.2   Google's street view gives you exactly that from http://maps.google .com

Google Maps, click on My Maps and then Create New Map. Check Google's Labs page for works in progress and recent releases. One of the best of the non-Googles is QuikMaps at http://quikmaps.geotripping.com.

WEBCAMS

The world never sleeps, or at least these cameras never do. We can check on the progress of the new Cronkite School building in downtown Phoenix by clicking on http://cronkite8building.asu.edu/. Webcams have been popular for monitoring weather, traffic, disasters, popular events and more. Not all are indexed, by far, but the databases grow all the time. Three places to search are Earthcam (www.earthcam.com), WebCamCentral (www.camcentral.com) and OnlineCamera (www.onlinecamera.com). Don't forget to see if local news sites (especially broadcast sites) have webcams; they've become increasingly popular.

BUILDING YOUR SOURCE FILE

The Rolodex was the mainstay of the newsroom. Every city desk, and the individual desks of all good reporters, held a well-worn flip-card index filled with names and numbers of sources. There is no replacement for a reporter's personalized Rolodex, but, on the Internet, there are several sites that are designed to help reporters find expert sources that may add to their source lists.

ProfNet, a subsidiary of PR Newswire, has a list of nearly 14,000 experts on a variety of topics, searchable by keyword at

   https://profnet.prnewswire.com

Sources and Experts. Kitty Bennett, news researcher at the *St. Petersburg Times*, compiled a one-stop Web site for reporters looking for expert sources on deadline. It is available at

   www.ibiblio.org/slanews/internet/experts.htm

The Poynter Institute compiles useful Web links on top news stories several times a month. The directory is available at

   http://poynteronline.org/column.asp?id=49

Organization Sites. The Casey Center on Families and Children maintains a carefully chosen database of speakers and experts. Check with other organizations to see what they have, too, when you need someone to address a specialized topic. Universities are excellent resources and many, if not most, have an organized experts service. You may wish to check faculty pages at specific schools, too, where CVs are often online.

Social Networking. With registration and a bit of connecting, a wide range of professionals can be found on LinkedIn.

Retired: The National Press Club experts database was a favorite for years. Sadly, no longer.

FREEDOM OF INFORMATION ACT

Journalists and others can file written requests under the Freedom of Information Act to pry information from uncooperative federal bureaucrats and agencies. Although it is used as a last resort by reporters, because of the response times that often drag into years, it remains a powerful tool of investigative reporting. Unfortunately, some reporters—we include ourselves—haven't been as aggressive in filing FOIA requests, in part because of the time delays and in part because it requires writing a formal letter citing the appropriate aspects of the law and finding the right people to send it to. Well, our friends at the Reporters Committee for Freedom of the Press, the Arlington, Va.–based nonprofit group devoted to aiding journalists in First Amendment battles for more than 35 years, have put together an online version of a FOIA request, complete with a fill-in-the-blanks form and the addresses of the various FOIA offices. It is located at

www.refp.org/foi_letter/generate.php

Fill in the blanks with your specific information, print it out and mail. As Jane Kirtley, former executive director of the Reporters Committee for Freedom of the Press, wrote: "The possibilities provided by the [Freedom of Information] Act are endless. All that is required is that journalists use it." The Reporters Committee also has put online its extraordinary "How to Use the Federal FOI Act." That is available at

www.rcfp.org/foiact/index.html

ACCESSING STATE AND LOCAL PUBLIC RECORDS

The Freedom of Information Act applies only to federal government agencies and records. State and local government records and meetings are covered by individual public record and open meeting laws in each state. And the laws vary widely from state to state. Ideally, all reporters should have a copy of these laws at their disposal and know how to use them. But in the reality of overburdened newsrooms, few editors and even fewer reporters know the details of their open meeting and public records law or even how to access them quickly.

Once again, the Reporters Committee for Freedom of the Press has provided an invaluable service to all journalists by putting on the Internet the full text of its comprehensive "Tapping Officials' Secrets" guides. These guides, one for each state, outline each law, including what information is public, how to obtain the information and how to appeal. The guides also detail how the law has been applied in the past. The Reporters Committee's guides specify whether the state laws cover electronic records, whether reporters can demand records in electronic form and whether electronic mail correspondence by public officials is covered under the statutes. Go to

www.rcfp.org/ogg/index.php

The Student Press Law Center has used the FOIA letter generator idea and created a similar site for state government public records requests for all 50 states. This is a tremendously powerful tool because both state and local government records must be requested under the state statutes. Go to

www.splc.org/foiletter.asp

The Reporters Committee also has put online a state-by-state breakdown of shield laws protecting reporters. The Reporter's Privilege compendium is at

http://rcfp.org/privilege

VITAL RECORDS

Records such as birth certificates, marriage licenses, and other vital records are available only in paper form, but vitalrec.com provides a listing of how to write for those records in all 50 states. It provides access to the Social Security Death Index, which is maintained by Ancestry.com, a genealogical firm, at

www.ancestry.com/search/db.aspx?dbid=3693&cj=1&o_xid=0001769
072&o_lid=0001769072&o_xt=22846411

It is easier to go through www.vitalrec.com.

MATH AID

Many people are drawn to journalism early in life in part because of the apparent lack of math required. But math-challenged reporters soon find out that basic calculations—means, percent changes, per capita spending, margin of error—come up every day in the newsroom. Robert Niles has developed "Statistics Every Writer Should Know," a user-friendly Web site that walks journalists through the minefield of mathematics. It is at

http://nilesonline.com/stats

If you want to take a quick refresher course online, sign up for News-University's free "Math for Journalists" taught by Debbie Wolfe, technology training officer for the St. Petersburg Times, at

www.newsu.org

Don't forget the calculator functions built into many search sites. In Google, for example, just type your math task (4+2) into the search bar and hit enter. Voila. The answer appears. For the "how-to," see

www.google.com/help/calculator

FAST FACTS

Full-text versions of several encyclopedias are available on the Internet, including the Columbia Encyclopedia at
www.bartleby.com/65 and InfoPlease, which combines almanacs with an encyclopedia, at
www.infoplease.com
The Congressional Research Service, the research arm of Congress, prepares succinct, nonpartisan briefing papers on most of the critical issues of the day for legislators and congressional aides. It is archived back through June 1999 at
http://fpc.state.gov/c4763.htm
Background on key issues also can be found at Public Agenda Online, a non-partisan research group. Public Agenda issue reports are available at
www.publicagenda.org
The Census Bureau's Statistical Abstract of the United States contains a wide range of statistics describing various social and economic aspects of the country. The latest version is available at
www.census.gov/compendia/statab
Need to get your hands quickly on a thumbnail sketch of the demographics of a particular country? Look it up in the CIA World Factbook at
www.cia.gov/library/publications/the-world-factbook/index.html

OTHER REFERENCE SOURCES

ConvertIt: calculators for measurements and time zones
www.convertit.com/Go/ConvertIt

Martindale's Calculators: wide selection
www.martindalecenter.com/Calculators.html

Bartlett's Familiar Quotations: www.bartleby.com/100/

Simpson's Contemporary Quotations: www.bartleby.com/63

Roget's Thesaurus: www.bartleby.com/62/

American Heritage Dictionary: www.bartleby.com/61/

and William Strunk Jr.'s classic, *The Elements of Style:*
www.bartleby.com/141/index.html

REFERENCE COLLECTIONS

CybertimesNavigator. Hundreds of reference links compiled for the newsroom of *The New York Times* and updated regularly. (Look up the site in a search engine if you're in a hurry.)

http://tech.nytimes.com/top/news/technology/
cybertimesnavigator/index.html

RefDesk. A one-stop site.
www.refdesk.org

CHAPTER 5

TOP DATA SITES
FOR NEWS STORIES

Much of what is found on federal, state, and local government Web sites is—from a journalistic perspective—garbage. They are filled largely with politicians stroking themselves and bureaucrats rationalizing their jobs. But between the puffery, reporters can find some of the best Web pages for news on government sites. In this chapter we will explore some of them. The focus here will be largely on the federal government because state, county and municipal government sites are different in each locale. We will, however, explore local and state government sites in more depth in Chapter 8, on building an electronic beat.

FEDERAL GOVERNMENT SITES, GENERAL

Census Bureau

If every government agency used the Census Bureau's Web site as a model, the Net would be a much happier place for reporters. The Census Bureau site can be used by reporters for everything from checking a simple statistical fact in a story and adding demographic background to an article to forming the basis for groundbreaking trend stories. The main Census Bureau address is
www.census.gov
The news section (www.census.gov/pubinfo/www/news.html) provides press releases—often embargoed—on the latest demographic, economic and cultural changes and trends. The releases are linked to the raw statistics, which often are broken down to the county level and include contact numbers for census specialists.
But press releases are just the beginning. Click on the Search box or go directly to www.census.gov/main/www/srchtool.html to get detailed information on a state, county, city or town from the latest census. Go to the U.S. Gazetteer (click on Geography) and call up any of hundreds of different variables on your community, from the number of Eskimos to the time people

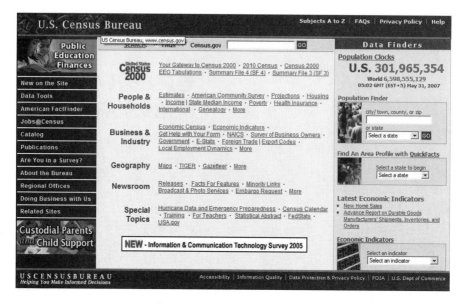

FIGURE 5.1   Home page of the U.S. Census Bureau at www.census.gov

leave for work to the number of bathrooms in the average home. Or click Map to get a tailored map of your community, with dozens of variables.

The Census Bureau also links users to the various state data centers around the country at

www.census.gov/sdc/www

If you had access to only one data site on the Web, this may be the one. Spend some time getting to know its powerful and easily accessible tools. Figure 5.1 illustrates the home page of the U.S. Census Bureau, which is valuable for background information, daily stories and trend pieces. Notice the "Population Clock," which provides up-to-the-second estimates of U.S. and worldwide populations.

Historic census data (from 1790 to 1970) on each state and county is available through the University of Virginia at

http://fisher.lib.virginia.edu/census

Federal Register

Every business day the federal government publishes a book that details each new regulation, proposed rule, announced hearing and every other administrative action taken by the executive branch of government the previous day. The Federal Register, however, traditionally has been used only by Beltway bureaucrats. Now the Register is online and searchable by keyword, giving local reporters around the country the power to find out how federal govern-

■ ■ ■ ■ ■ ▬▬▬▬▬▬▬▬▬▬▬▬▬▬▬▬▬▬▬▬▬▬▬▬▬▬▬▬▬▬▬

BOX 5.1

Paul Overberg of USA Today *relies heavily on the U.S. Census Bureau Web site.*

The bad news—and good news—about most Census Bureau reports is that they come straight at you. Unlike most numbers analysts in Washington, census experts are reluctant to analyze and cautious when they do.

That's what it was like in April 1997 when the Bureau published its regular set of estimates of each state's age breakdown. A bureau tip sheet told us it was coming, but not when. When the data appeared on the bureau's Web site, it was noted with a one-paragraph announcement.

Each state's file carried eight categories of race and Hispanic data for each sex for each year of age up to 85. That made 1,360 data cells for each state, times six years, times 50 states, plus the District of Columbia.

You'd no sooner approach such a data pile without a plan than you would an interview with President Clinton. Our demographics reporter, Haya El Nasser, and I had talked about several ideas, and we had tried an old version of this data.

The one that worked best was showing where baby boomers had moved as they reached middle age in the 1990s. The states where they cluster are different than where they did in 1990, when they had different priorities, and the nation a different set of regional economic circumstances.

Without the Web and a spreadsheet, a deadline story like this was unthinkable. With both, it was a matter of a couple hours of sifting to pull out a customized slice of ages and measure its share in each state. Then El Nasser hit the phones with solid news that helped to draw quotes from demographers who were themselves curious about what we had found.

One unanticipated bonus: The Census Bureau had computed and tucked in each state's file its estimated median age for each year. Pulling these out, we saw that West Virginia had crept up on Florida and actually passed it to claim the oldest population in 1996. This surprised editors and became a nice paragraph for the story's roundup of trends.

ment executive branch decisions are affecting their communities. Take a look at the leads of these stories, which were produced by University of Maryland students writing for the College of Journalism's Capital News Service public affairs reporting program. The genesis of each story came from obscure references in the Federal Register found in a single Internet search.

Melissa Corley's story was published in the Baltimore *Sun,* and other Maryland papers:

> Sunbathers perched atop military firing targets in the Chesapeake Bay have prompted the Navy to push for tougher restrictions at the firing range, Pentagon officials said.

Nicole Gill's article ran in the *Washington Times* and the Baltimore *Sun:*

SILVER SPRING—Two dozen historic buildings at the Walter Reed Army Medical Center are in such disrepair that the Pentagon is considering ripping down or selling off the structures.

The Forest Glen Annex buildings, which served as a women's finishing school from the late 19th century until World War II, go largely unused and are too expensive to maintain, Army officials say.

Steven Kreytak wrote this feature, which appeared in several newspapers on Maryland's Eastern Shore:

They have prowled the depths of the Chesapeake Bay since dinosaurs roamed the earth, but for the last 30 years the shortnose sturgeon have been on the verge of extinction.

In fact, up until this year, scientists believed there were none left in the bay. But fishermen found three shortnose sturgeons in their nets in April, renewing the hopes of scientists and environmentalists alike.

And now, government scientists are launching a study they hope will show that the three shortnose sturgeons found this spring represent the remnants of a Chesapeake Bay population and not just stray visitors from the nearby Delaware River.

Sunny Kaplan wrote a series of features for the *Sun* on historic sites placed on the National Register of Historic Places.

The Federal Register is probably one of the worst-looking sites out there. And reporters have to poke through quite a bit of bureaucratese to find the nuggets of news. But it is also one of the most valuable Internet sites for producing original local news. Give it a try by looking at the last few months of the Federal Register, using the town or county that you cover as keywords. Other good keywords include local waterways, utilities, companies, military installations and hospitals.

The Federal Register, dating back to 1995 on the Internet, is located within the Government Printing Office site. Go there directly at

www.gpoaccess.gov/fr/index.html

Congress

The Thomas site, named for Thomas Jefferson, includes full texts of all U.S. House and Senate legislation, the *Congressional Record* and Index, e-mail addresses for lawmakers, legislators' directories, committee assignments, the U.S. Constitution, Declaration of Independence, congressional ethics manual and other resources. This site also has jumping off points to the Code of Federal Regulations and U.S. Code. It is located at

http://thomas.loc.gov

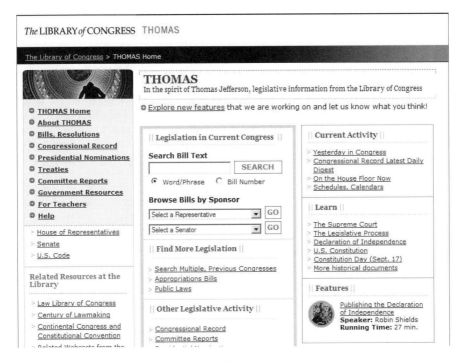

FIGURE 5.2   Library of Congress at http://thomas.loc.gov

The Thomas congressional site (see Figure 5.2) allows local reporters to monitor their legislators' work in Washington.

Project Vote Smart has a wealth of information on lawmakers and their voting records.

www.vote-smart.org/index.phtml

More than 30 special-interest groups' ratings of lawmakers are linked through Voter Information Services at

www.vis.org

And the Center for Responsive Politics has a database on congressional travel, searchable by lawmaker, special-interest group sponsor or destination.

www.opensecrets.org/travel

Government Documents

The Government Printing Office provides the federal budget, congressional bills, presidential documents, the Federal Register, the Congressional Record, the U.S. Government Manual and other government documents the day of publication.

www.access.gpo.gov

Government Statistics

Fedstats links to statistics from more than 100 federal agencies.

www.fedstats.gov

Federal Audits

Each major agency of the federal government has an inspector general's office that conducts investigations and audits of the department and federal programs that the agency oversees. This site, at www.ignet.gov, brings you to IG reports throughout the federal government.

Other Federal Agencies

Auburn University hosts the Federal Web Locator, a site linking to all federal agencies and programs, at

www.lib.auburn.edu/madd/docs/fedloc.html

Congressional Investigations

The General Accounting Office, the investigative arm of Congress, has new reports available on the Internet within days of their release. GAO reports help background issues for enterprise stories.

www.gao.gov

Library of Congress

This system includes brief descriptions and the status of all bills and resolutions in the U.S. Congress, past and present. It also includes the Library of Congress card catalog, which is useful for identifying potential expert sources for a particular topic. It also has select Congressional Research Service reports, which, like GAO reports, are useful for backgrounding issues. Reach the Library of Congress at

http://lcweb.loc.gov

Lobbyists

The Center for Responsive Politics, a nonprofit watchdog group, provides a database of congressional lobbyists, searchable by lobbyist, company, or industry. The site, which also includes annual expenditures by lobbyists, is available at

www.opensecrets.org/lobbyists/index.asp

POLITICS AND CAMPAIGNS

Find and research elected officials.

> *USA.gov:* Contact information from the government's Web portal. www.usa.gov/Contact/Elected.shtml
>
> *Congress.org:* governors, legislators, more. Search by ZIP, last name or state. www.congress.org/congressorg/dbq/officials/?lvl=L
>
> *Congressional Biographical Directory,* 1774–present. http://bioguide.congress.gov/biosearch/biosearch.asp

Campaign Ads

> *Election TV:* a nonpartisan site that also has top election blogs. www.election.tv
>
> *American Museum of the Moving Image:* presidential campaign commercials back to 1952. http://livingroomcandidate.movingimage.us/
>
> *MSNBC Campaign Ad Watch 2004* (check back for 2008 campaign) http://www.msnbc.msn.com/id/4647288/
>
> *Ease History.* Ads and topical analysis. www.easehistory.org/index2.html
>
> *Archive Collection.* Presidential, gubernatorial and other campaigns. http://faculty.kutztown.edu/richards/220/ad-archive.html

Federal Campaign Finances

Political Money Line, begun in 1995 by Kent Cooper and Tony Raymond, was acquired by Congressional Quarterly in 2006. Reporters can find out how much money their local congressional or Senate candidates spent on a particular race or how much money they raised. But that's only the beginning. Political Money Line allows reporters to easily determine who in their community are the biggest campaign contributors, which communities give the most and which local special-interest groups are the most generous with their campaign dollars. The founders continue to operate the site at

> www.politicalmoneyline.com/

Other helpful federal campaign finance sites include the Center for Responsive Politics (www.opensecrets.org) and the Federal Election Commission (www.fec.gov/disclosure.shtml).

BOX 5.2

Bill Loving was the computer-assisted reporting editor at the Minneapolis Star Tribune *when he combined a tip from an Internet discussion group, Web data and a spreadsheet analysis to develop a story on tornado patterns in Minnesota.*

The *Minneapolis Star Tribune*'s computer-assisted reporting story on tornadoes in June 1997 is a good example of the power of the Internet as a reporting tool: The story idea itself actually originated in an Internet discussion group and then was carried out with data downloaded from a Web site. This also shows the most powerful application of the Internet for journalists, in my opinion: access to searchable or downloadable databases online.

Sometime in 1996 I noticed a message posted to NICAR-L, the e-mail discussion group hosted by National Institute for Computer-Assisted Reporting, from a reporter who had technical questions about converting historical tornado data into maps. I took note of the existence of the tornado data, which was stored at a Web site, and put it on my list of future story ideas.

In the spring of 1997, as Minnesota's tornado season approached, I went back to that Web site, maintained by the Storm Prediction Center in Oklahoma (www.spc.noaa.gov), clicked my way to the on-line archive section and downloaded the data on Minnesota tornadoes from 1950 through 1995. (There are tables for each of the 50 states, plus one for the entire country.) The download was quite simple: The data table was stored as a compressed "zip" file, which I downloaded in Netscape Navigator simply by clicking on a link to the file. I also downloaded the accompanying record layout file.

After unzipping the data file with WinZip, I opened it into the Microsoft Excel spreadsheet program. Voilà: In a few minutes I had an Excel table of 858 reported tornadoes, including the dates and times, intensity ratings, damage levels, deaths and injuries and, best of all, the latitude and longitude coordinates of the tornadoes' paths. That meant that the tornadoes could indeed be mapped with GIS mapping software, which takes databases containing geographic location fields and converts them to maps.

I went to the *Star Tribune* science editor, Josephine Marcotty, and suggested a story on tornadoes for our weekly Science page. She was excited about the idea, and assigned it to science writer Jim Dawson and scheduled it for early June, the beginning of Minnesota's peak season for twisters.

Because I knew I would want to group and sum the tornado data by various measures, rather than just sorting and filtering, I imported the Excel table into Microsoft Access database software, which I find easier and more powerful for such operations. I exported the resulting summary data back into Excel and created some charts for the reporter on most common dates and times-of-day for tornadoes, and so on. Then I exported the data into Arcview, a mapping program, which was able to read the latitude and longitude data and plot the location of each tornado on a map of Minnesota.

The maps and several charts were published on the Science page as part of a package of stories on tornado season, just a couple of weeks after the idea was first proposed.

State Campaign Finances

The National Institute on Money in State Politics has available a database of state campaign finance records for selected states, searchable by candidate, individual donor, or one of 115 special-interest groups. The institute has data from all 50 states. The database for the nonpartisan National Institute on Money in State Politics is available at

> www.followthemoney.org

Campaign Finance Stories

The Campaign Finance Information Center at Investigative Reporters and Editors provides a database of campaign finance story ideas and tip sheets contributed by political journalists nationwide. It is available at

> www.campaignfinance.org/stories.html

State Lawmakers and Lobbyists

> The Center for Public Integrity: Private finances.
>
> www.publicintegrity.org/oi/
>
> Lobbyist Register
>
> www.kssos.org/forms/elections/lobdir.pdf

Political News

The Internet is an excellent way to keep up on campaign finance news. Some of the best sites include

> *Multimedia archives* in Yahoo! News Full Coverage
>
> http://news.yahoo.com/fc/US/US_Electoral_Process
>
> Washington Post's On Politics
>
> www.washingtonpost.com/wp-dyn/content/politics/index.html
>
> Campaigns and Elections
>
> www.campaignline.com/
>
> CQ Politics Online
>
> www.cqpolitics.com/
>
> CNN Politics
>
> www.cnn.com/POLITICS/
>
> The Caucus: Political Blogging from *The New York Times*
>
> www.nytimes.com/pages/politics/index.html

Taegan Goddard's Political Wire
  http://politicalwire.com/
MSNBC National Journal/Politics
  http://www.msnbc.msn.com/id/14016001/
YouTube News and Politics (videos)
  http://youtube.com/categories_portal?c=25&e=1

Polls and Parties

PollingReport.com provides synopses of recent polls, by issue.
  www.pollingreport.com

Other polls available online include:

Gallup: www.gallup.com
Roper: www.ropercenter.uconn.edu

And don't overlook the Pew Research Center for People and the Press:
  www.people-press.org/index.htm

The major political parties are also helpful resources. The Democratic National Committee (www.democrats.org) and the Republican National Committee (www.rnc.org) each has its own Web site. The national parties also provide links to state and county party Web sites as well as other party arms such as the committees for House, Senate and gubernatorial campaigns. The partisan sites are important not only for information on the parties and individual candidates, but also to analyze how politicians are using the Internet as part of the campaigning process.

These days, the online presence of candidates is important to watch as well. Check their home pages, official pages (if any) and "fan" pages, and search on YouTube for campaign videos.

HEALTH AND SAFETY

Toxic Emissions

The Right-to-Know Network makes available the government's Toxic Release Inventory, which enables reporters to pinpoint toxic emissions from specific plants. It is searchable by company or geographic location and details the type and quantity of toxic emissions. RTK Net includes other environmental databases.
  www.rtknet.org

Highway Safety

The Transportation Department's Fatality Analysis Reporting System includes data on all fatal vehicle accidents in the United States, searchable by state and county. Accident information also is broken down by age of drivers, incidence of alcohol, and speeding. It is located at

> www.fars.nhtsa.dot.gov

Aviation Safety

The Federal Aviation Administration offers a series of databases that includes government reports on aviation accidents, near collisions, traffic and capacity statistics, and other safety reports. The safety data is available at

> www.faa.gov/data_statistics

A commercial service, Landings, makes available aircraft registration and ownership information, searchable by owner name or registration number.

> www.landings.com (click on databases)

Railroad Safety

The Federal Railroad Administration provides a database with accident and inspection reports, broken down by county.

> http://safetydata.fra.dot.gov/OfficeofSafety

Medical Library

PubMed, a database of more than 17 million references to articles published in more than 4,000 medical journals back to the 1950s, is made available through the National Library of Medicine at the National Institutes of Health.

> www.ncbi.nlm.nih.gov/PubMed

Doctors

The Association of State Medical Board Executives links to data from state medical boards, which provide data on licensed doctors, including their specialties, medical school, license number and whether there is regulatory action pending.

> www.docboard.org

National Center for Health Statistics

A wide array of NCHS data and statistics are available through the Centers for Disease Control at

> www.cdc.gov/nchs

BOX 5.3

Ernie Slone, as computer-assisted reporting editor at the Orange County Register, *explains how he used the Internet to figure out how tax dollars are spent.*

Promise that it will last; but in this world nothing is certain but death and taxes.
—Benjamin Franklin

The world hasn't changed much since Franklin wrote those words two centuries ago. Come April and many of your neighbors will be thinking about that check they will have to send off to Uncle Sam. And you can bet they will grouse about it—with good reason.

Federal, state and local taxes in 1997 claimed 38 percent of the income of a median two-earner U.S. family (making $54,910), up from 37.3 percent in 1996. That is more than they spend on food (8.9 percent), clothing (3.7 percent), housing (15.3 percent) and transportation (6.6 percent), combined. The tax burden, adjusted for inflation, is at historic highs.

While reporters and editors often give the average Jane or José in-depth consumer analysis on how much they pay for meat or autos or mortgages, we seldom tell that typical family what they are getting for the $22,521 in taxes they spent in 1997. Too often we lapse into the uninformative cliché: how long was the line at the post office or why did you wait until the last minute?

By pulling data from the Internet, or getting it via e-mail, you can penetrate the unknown, telling your readers with enlightening accuracy how much they spend on federal taxes, how much comes back to their area and who benefits. You also can tell them how good a job the government is doing in catching those who dodge their responsibilities.

Here is how the *Orange County Register* tells those stories to its readers:

FEDERAL SPENDING DATA
Each year in mid-April the Census Bureau posts Consolidated Federal Fund reports, basically how and where the government spent its money for the fiscal year. The data are available yearlong on the Internet, a great resource for stories about such issues as the decline of military spending. But here's an insider's tip: By contacting the Census folks in advance you can get them to e-mail or express mail you the latest detailed data on your area, usually in early April, plus the state and national summaries. Then, when April 15 rolls around, you are ready to print or broadcast a tax profile with the latest information. The address is
www.census.gov/govs/www

Click on Federal Government Data. (You will note that the site also offers detailed data on state tax collections, state government finances, etc.)

To make sense of the numbers you will need an understanding of relational databases, which can take one list and match it up with another. (This is a good early-learning project to begin developing those skills.) When you download the data, make sure you get two reference files to convert codes in the detail data files to more descriptive text:

- The Program Identification File contains program identification codes and names.
- The Agency File contains federal agency identification codes and names.

The dollars include grants to local government, salaries and wages of federal employees in your area, direct payments to individuals for programs such as Social Security and federal procurement contracts.

The Register also adds payments Orange County receives for Medicaid and Aid to Families with Dependent Children, which don't show up in the Census numbers. Those amounts are readily available from the two federal agencies.

The data are only the beginning, leading you to fascinating stories behind the numbers. In 1996 the federal government spent $215,265 in our county to bury veterans, and $435,582 for a "talent search" to find poor kids who might make it in college. We told stories of individuals, how a disabled veteran's life has been turned around thanks to government grants and how a professor is stretching $13,510 in research funds to try to save endangered forests in Southern California.

It will make your readers and viewers wonder if too much money is spent on some things, and not enough on others.

FEDERAL TAX DATA

In 1996 Orange County sent $15.9 billion to Washington, but got back only about $10 billion, one of the biggest deficits among California counties. (No wonder we had that bankruptcy thing.)

To find out how much your county or city is shipping to the feds contact the Tax Foundation. The foundation is a nonprofit, nonpartisan policy research organization that has monitored fiscal issues at the federal, state and local levels since 1937. Its online site is at

www.taxfoundation.org

The site provides dozens of detailed tables, listing tax burden by state, how much a typical family pays, when "tax freedom" day occurs each year and so forth. But for the really detailed information on your local area, you need to contact the foundation and request those numbers. Staffers are very responsive, but typically need a couple of days to send it.

In 1996 each of our county's 2.6 million residents sent an average of $6,000 to Uncle Sam, a tenth of all the federal tax dollars collected in the Golden State.

TAX ENFORCEMENT

If we are so generous, that must mean few Orange Countians are fudging on their taxes, right? Don't tell that to the IRS. In 1996 Southern California residents were audited at the second-highest rate in the country. Who got audited more, you ask? Those reckless devils across the desert in Las Vegas, of course.

But while auditors looked very closely at our records, federal prosecutors took a different view. The federal district that includes our county was among the lowest in the country for referring, prosecuting and convicting tax criminals, and the few who were convicted received only 8.3 months in the federal slammer, compared with a national average of double that term. (When we wrote that story the federal prosecutor complained that he would like to pursue more cheaters, but doesn't have the staff.)

You can tell your readers and viewers how your area rates on audits and tax enforcement by accessing the data from Syracuse University's Transactional Records Access Clearinghouse at

trac.syr.edu

While the data are there, free for the taking, none of these stories will get done without planning and initiative. Remember that other quote from old Ben Franklin: "God helps them that help themselves."

CRIME AND PUNISHMENT

U.S. Circuit Courts of Appeals

The U.S. Circuit Courts of Appeals are by far the most undercovered courts in the country. Big federal cases are covered aggressively when in U.S. District Court, but often disappear when they are appealed and go to the next level—the Circuit Courts. That is in large part because the Circuit Courts often are out of the newspapers' reach. For instance, the 4th Circuit Court, which covers federal appeals from Maryland, is in Richmond, Va., about three hours south of Baltimore. Newspapers traditionally have relied on local wire coverage, but the wires usually only cover the court sporadically. Now, the geographic problem no longer exists because the full-text opinions of all 11 Circuit Courts of Appeals are available on the Internet. The Emory University School of Law has links to the rulings at

> www.law.emory.edu/FEDCTS

A quick check each day of your Circuit Court can provide good breaking stories that the competition doesn't have. How many stories? Well, Capital News Service reporters covering the 4th Circuit Court via the Web for Maryland daily newspapers had eight articles published by a wide variety of Maryland daily newspapers over the course of one semester (12 weeks). Their stories ranged from a murder-for-hire death sentence appeal and an illegal alien smuggling case to an age discrimination suit and a claim by a federal scientist that his colleagues were trying to destroy his reputation.

U.S. Supreme Court

While the wires cover Supreme Court rulings much more comprehensively than they cover the Circuit Courts, you may want to expand on coverage of high court rulings that come from your area. The Cornell University Law School has full-text U.S. Supreme Court decisions available the day of release at

> http://supct.law.cornell.edu/supct

The Cornell Law site has opinions dating back to 1990 as well as historic cases. For older Supreme Court cases (opinions from 1937 through 1975), go to

> www.fedworld.gov

For cases dating to 1893, visit FindLaw.

> www.findlaw.com/casecode/supreme.html

U.S. District Courts and Bankruptcy Courts

Many Federal District Courts and Federal Bankruptcy Courts are online with full-text opinions. To check your local federal courts (see Figure 5.3), go to

> www.uscourts.gov/allinks.html

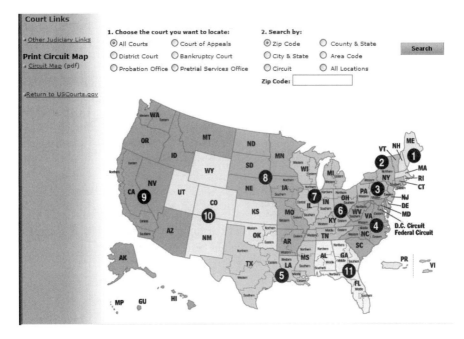

FIGURE 5.3   U.S. Courts Interactive Map at www.uscourts.gov

Securities Cases

The Stanford University School of Law has full-text complaints, summaries and briefs on securities class action complaints.

> http://securities.stanford.edu

Federal Laws and Regulations

The National Archives and Records Administration provides full text of the Federal Register, Code of Federal Regulations, Public Laws, presidential orders and other federal legal sources.

> www.gpoaccess.gov/nara/index.html

Legal Directory

West Legal Directory contains thumbnail profiles of more than 800,000 U.S. law firms and attorneys. It is searchable by name, state, town, type of law, college attended, and other factors.

> http://directory.findlaw.com   or   http://lawyers.findlaw.com

Crime Statistics and Sources

The FBI's Uniform Crime Reports are available at

www.fbi.gov/ucr/ucr.htm

A wide array of federal statistics on crime and justice is available through the Bureau of Justice Statistics' Sourcebook of Criminal Justice Statistics. The sourcebook is made available by the State University of New York at Albany.

www.albany.edu/sourcebook

Sex Offender Registries

There is great variation in the information provided by the many search sites available. Some post photographs and explicit details of crimes. Some post interactive maps to show where convicted offenders live.

The FBI's site provides links to state registries.

www.fbi.gov/hq/cid/cac/states.htm

The United States Department of Justice maintains the Dru Sjodan National Sex Offender Registry Public Website.

www.nsopr.gov/

Parents for Megan's Law

www.parentsformeganslaw.com/html/links.lasso

Family Watchdog is searchable in English and Spanish.

www.familywatchdog.us/

BUSINESS AND NONPROFITS

Securities and Exchange Commission

The SEC Edgar database is a repository for documents filed at the SEC. Reporters can access 10Ks, 13Ds, proxies and other vital corporate documentation. It is probably the most important site for business reporters, but also is valuable for local reporters who want to go beyond press release reporting on the utilities and big employers in their circulation area. The Edgar database was one of the first on the Web to provide full-text documents and remains one of the most journalistically powerful. It goes back to 1994 and links up-to-the-minute filings.

www.sec.gov/cgi-bin/srch-edgar

SECInfo provides e-mail alerts on new filings and indexes more than 1 billion links with the U.S. SEC and Canadian CSA filings.

www.secinfo.com

Corporation Profiles and Press Releases

Hoover's, Inc. offers a searchable database that provides useful details on many companies. Each company listing includes Web and mail addresses, a thumbnail profile, competitors, stock quotes, the company's press releases, news stories mentioning the company, SEC filings, and annual reports.

www.hoovers.com

Business-related press releases are available through Business Wire

www.businesswire.com

and PR NewsWire at

http://prnewswire.com

State Corporation Records

The National Association of Secretaries of State site links to 50 U.S. Secretary of State offices, which regulate corporations and charities. You'll find bios, contact information and job descriptions among the useful pages.

www.nass.org/sos/sos.html

Property Records

The University of Virginia provides links to the growing number of state, county and municipal governments that provide property records online.

http://indorgs.virginia.edu/portico/personalproperty.html

Nonprofits

The Prospector provides links to state and national charity databases.

www.internet-prospector.org/charities.htm

GuideStar includes millions of I-990 forms filed by charities that report $25,000 or more in earnings.

www.guidestar.org

Foundation Finder is a staple in development offices.

www.foundationcenter.org

Workplace Safety

The Occupational Safety and Health Administration provides a database of workplace inspection reports, violations, and fines, searchable by institution.

> www.osha.gov/oshstats

Census Bureau Economic Data

The Census Bureau provides a wide array of economic and business data, broken down by industries and regions, including annual county business patterns, leading economic indicators and statistics on income, poverty, and labor.

> www.census.gov/econ/www/index.html

The Census Bureau's CenStats site provides business patterns by county and ZIP code, monthly building permit data, federal spending, Census tract data and more.

> http://censtats.census.gov

Banking Records

The Federal Deposit Insurance Corp. provides data on all FDIC-insured institutions, including total assets and deposits, and aggregated data for states, counties and metropolitan areas.

> www.fdic.gov/bank/index.html

Patents

The U.S. Patent and Trademark Office has a searchable database with all U.S. patents since 1790.

> www.uspto.gov/patft

Business News

Use the Internet to keep up with the latest breaking news on the business beat. Top business news sites include Reuters (www.reuters.com), the Associated Press business wire via the *Washington Post* (www.washingtonpost.com/wp-dyn/business/latestap), Bloomberg (www.bloomberg.com) and CNN Money (http://money.cnn.com).

New York Times Business Guide

Rich Meislin of the *New York Times* has put together a comprehensive guide to dozens of Web sites useful to the business reporter. Find the Business Navigator at

> www.nytimes.com/ref/business/business-navigator.html

■ ■ ■ ■ ■

BOX 5.4

Penny Loeb was a senior editor at U.S. News & World Report *when she used a state government database on the Internet to help her nail down a story about coal mining.*

"Shear Madness" was the headline for my investigation of a kind of coal mining in West Virginia known as mountaintop removal. The mines literally take up to 500 feet off the top to get at multiple coal seams. Much of the top of the mountain ends up in the valleys below. During the process, residents' homes are damaged by blasting, and their wells dry up. Even entire communities are being eliminated.

When I started the project, I asked state environmental officials how much of the mountains were being mined. They couldn't tell me. No acreage seemed to exist in paper reports. Every large surface mine has several permits, and these do have acreage. But nobody seemed to have added up the acreage.

I was going to accept what state officials told me. We were using our own estimations from flying over the mines. These were confirmed by the state official who flew with us. We said about 15 percent of the mountains in southern West Virginia had been mined.

A lot of lucky things happened to me on this story. And this is one. About a month before publication, I was looking at the maps of coal mines on the Web site for the state Division of Environmental Protection. (This agency has one of the best Web sites I've seen for a government.) I thought I could download a map for our art department. In trying to open the map after downloading, I noticed I had gotten a.dbf file. I like those. I opened it up. It was all the individual permits, with acreage. All I had to do was add up the acreage for surface mines. It came to about 323,000 acres. My editor liked square miles better: 512 square miles. Unfortunately the database couldn't count the number of mountains being cut off.

And here is the newspaper's business site

www.nytimes.com/pages/business/index.html

STATE AND LOCAL GOVERNMENTS

Most states can be reached at www.state.??.us, with the question marks standing for the two-initial state abbreviation. Many state agencies can be reached at www.???.state.??.us, with the first set of question marks representing the agency's abbreviation and the second set representing the two-initial state abbreviation. For instance, the New York State Department of Transportation would be www.dot.state.ny.us.

Most county governments can be found at www.co.???.??.us, where the first question marks represent the county name and the second set represents the state abbreviation. For instance, www.co.fairfax.va.us is Fairfax County, Virginia.

Many city governments can be found at www.ci.???.??.us, where the first set of question marks represents the name of the city and the second set represents the two-initial abbreviation for the state. For example, www.ci.boston.ma.us is the address for Boston, Mass.

A number of sites provide links to government sites. These are among the most useful and comprehensive.

Global Computing
www.globalcomputing.com/StatesContent.htm

SLGN Directory links to more than 11,250 Web sites.
www.statelocalgov.net/index.cfm

Note that some local sites are quite complex. The one for Westchester County, N.Y., for example, has videos of press conferences and announcements and links to news and multimedia reports.

INTERNATIONAL

An extensive archive exists at Northwestern University. One that links to documents of official governments is at

www.library.northwestern.edu/govinfo/resource/internat/foreign.html

Unrepresented nations and people's organizations are linked at
www.unpo.org/

Yahoo Search has an extensive list of links.

http://dir.yahoo.com/Government/Countries/

World Statesmen provides current and past information about leaders of nations and territories.

www.worldstatesmen.org/

Central Intelligence Agency's World Leaders carries regularly updated information on chiefs of state and Cabinet members of foreign governments.

www.cia.gov/library/publications/world-leaders-1/index.html

CIA's World Fact Book is a prime reference for an immense amount of information and should be in every reporter and editor's bookmarks.

www.cia.gov/library/publications/the-world-factbook/index.html

The University of Michigan maintains a library reference site for international organizations and related information.

www.lib.umich.edu/govdocs/intl.html

CHAPTER 6

ONLINE NEWS PUBLICATIONS

GROWTH OF ONLINE NEWSPAPERS

Shortly after the birth of the World Wide Web came a flood of online news publications as newspapers and magazines—fearful of becoming anachronisms—rushed to publish online. By fall 2001, there were more than 4,000 newspapers on the Internet in the United States alone, according to the *American Journalism Review.* Around 2002, the Web popped. Fewer and fewer newspapers treated their online editions as places to "shovel" their print content—as had been the practice when newspapers first staked their claims in the unknown and still wild virtual frontier of the 1990s. Rather, online news sites began to come into their own with original as well as shared and archived content, creating a bonanza for reporters looking for information. The downside? More deadline pressure. With news sites "always on," the 24/7 news expectation was born and "feeding the beast" raised practical as well as ethical challenges to ensuring accuracy as well as speed. In 2006, the Pew Research Center reported, 31 percent of people regularly got their news online, an upward change of 8 percentage points from six years earlier. The search for a business model continues even as the industry looks to deliver individualized news through a variety of technological devices. Whatever the future, it's clear the Internet will continue to be a valuable reporting resource for all journalists. Let's explore how.

REGIONAL AND STATEWIDE NEWSPAPERS

Most parts of the country have a dominant regional or statewide newspaper. In Massachusetts, it is the *Boston Globe.* Illinois has the *Chicago Tribune.* In California, it is the *Los Angeles Times.* Keeping close tabs on the dominant regional paper allows local reporters to compare their coverage to the larger regional competition and can provide story ideas that can be localized. In the past, those papers often were not easily accessible at outer distribution areas.

Now, of course, they are instantly available online. There, viewers also get Web-only content and breaking news. Some sites offer an extra "electronic" version of the print edition—somewhat like a glorified photocopy with search tools. You can see how the newspaper "played" a story, access inside pages and see content not included in the online version. However, it's a day behind the online news and rarely free beyond a one-time trial. Still, one time might be all you need. See newsstand.com for a list of many available e-papers or check a specific paper's home page. Several Web sites offer links to newspapers around the country. *American Journalism Review*'s News Sources are searchable by media type:

> Newspapers: www.ajr.org/Newspapers.asp?MediaType=1
>
> Network TV affiliates: www.ajr.org/Newspapers.asp?MediaType=3

The Newspaper Association of America's NewsVoyager links to local papers at

> www.newspaperlinks.com/home.cfm

For more than 250 community papers (and a scanned archive dating from 1865), see Small Town Papers at

> www.smalltownpapers.com/

The Newseum showcases hundreds of newspapers, local through international, and organizes them geographically as well as alphabetically. Each day, an image of the newspaper's current front page is linked to its home site.

> www.newseum.org/todaysfrontpages/default.asp

NATIONAL AND TOPICAL COVERAGE

Online news sites originate from more than one kind of news organization, including online-only. Newspaper, magazine, broadcast and new-media organizations spawned Web giants as varied as nytimes.com, washingtonpost .com, msnbc.com, slate and YahooNews.

Reading major publications often can provide story ideas that can be localized for your community. Also, following publications that excel in coverage of your issue beat can provide you with important background information as well as keep you current. For instance, political reporters may want to keep up with the *Washington Post*. Reporters covering high technology issues may want to read the *San Jose Mercury News*. Higher education reporters may want to look at the *Boston Globe*. Reporters covering elderly issues might look to the *St. Petersburg Times*. You also may want to keep tabs on the work of a specific reporter who is well known for covering your topic.

The layout of most online publications makes it easy to search for issue-based coverage. Navigation links are usually topical (business, food, politics, etc.) and lead to pages devoted to those subjects. Issue pages—or

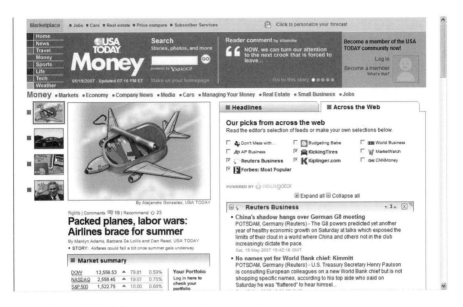

FIGURE 6.1   USA Today money page from usatoday.com

(Reprinted with permission of USATODAY.com. All rights reserved.)

"shells"—are "jump-off" pages for current and archived stories as well as "go-to" pages for related tools, resource links and contextual material (see Figure 6.1). During a spot-check for this book, USAToday.com's Money page included 57 sublinks from the top-bar headings, access to 10 business feeds, headline links to 31 current stories, several market surveys, a quote search, two market trackers, two currency converters, a gas-price tracker, a payment calculator, searchable car reviews and a site index with 45 links. Unlike print packages, issue pages are deep and wide beyond what you see. They work if you're mining info for one story or building knowledge over time. More about that in Chapter 8.

OUT-OF-STATE PUBLICATIONS

There are local stories that have strong out-of-town connections. One of the best examples is that of a high-profile official in one location being considered for a job, or hired for a job, in another location. For instance, the president of Ohio State University left to become president of Brown University in Providence, Rhode Island, and the president of the University of Maryland at College Park, William Kirwan, was hired to take over the Ohio State post. The Kirwan story was big news not only in Maryland, where he was leaving, but in Ohio. And papers in both towns were competing for the story before it

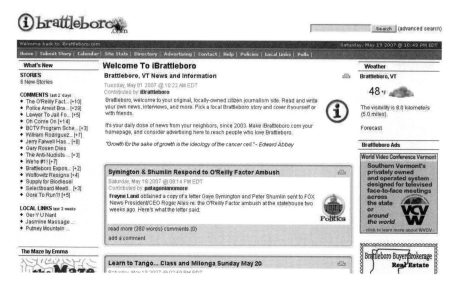

FIGURE 6.2   Home page for iBrattleboro.com

(Reprinted with permission of iBrattleboro.com)

was officially announced. Not long ago, a Maryland reporter would not have had easy access to the *Columbus Dispatch* and other Ohio papers covering the Kirwan story, just as the Ohio reporters would have a tough time getting hold of that day's Baltimore *Sun.* But now those papers can be easily accessed on the Web along with their archives.

CITIZEN JOURNALISM

Among the biggest changes in the past few years is the tremendous growth of grassroots or participatory journalism fueling a burgeoning emphasis on intensely local coverage. Many observers peg the tragedies of Sept. 11, 2001, as a turning point in Web journalism. Other disasters—the London bombing, the Asian tsunami, Hurricane Katrina—reinforced the Internet as a way for people to connect, learn news first-hand and contribute to history-in-a-hurry in large and small ways. The Monday of the Virginia Tech massacre, hits on CNN's Exchange (its site for user-generated content) increased 2,063 percent from Sunday, according to an Internet analysis service. A now-famous video shot with a cell phone camera by a student was taken before journalists could get to the remote crime scene, but it's part of the journalistic record.

In less than a decade, Web sites dedicated to community concerns and "staffed" by citizen volunteers cropped up along with user-friendly technology. Societal benefits aside, journalists gained a rich, new venue for learning about people and places, locating sources, asking questions, getting answers and finding stories that fly below established media's radar. Among the most successful community sites are iBrattleboro.com (Vermont), WestportNow.com (Connecticut) and the Backfence.com sites (Maryland, Virginia, California, Illinois). The Center for Media and Democracy links to many such sites at www. sourcewatch.org/index.php?title=List_of_citizen_journalism_websites.

TRADE AND SPECIALTY PUBLICATIONS

Daily, weekly and monthly newsletters and magazines that specialize in a single topic are valuable tools for daily beat reporters. The best of these special-interest publications cover stories in-depth, and often break news before the mass circulation newspapers and magazines. For instance, when one of the authors was covering defense issues in Washington, *Defense Week* was on his must-read list because it broke stories that affected his readers, and most of his readers were not subscribers to the pricey newsletter. Many of these publications are available on the Web. Some of the publications will make available only parts of stories or full versions of only some of their stories but even those sites are useful to reporters who can then get the full-text versions of the stories of particular interest.

To find the right publications for your beat, try MediaFinder, which offers searchable directories of newsletters and magazines. MediaFinder is located at

www.mediafinder.com

NEWSPAPER ARCHIVES

A weakness of the Web is in accessing past newspaper stories. Most newspapers that have electronic archives charge a fee after a brief free period. *Washington Post* researcher Margot Williams created a Web site that details the costs of the various archives and how far back the articles go in many U.S. newspapers. Special Libraries Association volunteers maintain it at

www.ibiblio.org/slanews/internet/archives.html

Search engines are incorporating story archives into their databases. Google's archive results are accompanied by a timeline that helps place the news in context.

http://news.google.com/archivesearch?tab=wn

NEWS AGGREGATORS

Two of the best known automated portals are GoogleNews and YahooNews. Search robots crawl thousands of Web sources for stories and display the top ones on a page that updates frequently. Both of these sites are searchable and provide ways to focus the results (Full Coverage for Yahoo).

Google: news.google.com/
Yahoo: news.yahoo.com/

SOCIAL NETWORK SITES

When reporters at *Collegiate Times,* Virginia Tech's newspaper, needed to know who was alive and who was not after the Blacksburg campus shootings in April 2007, they turned to Facebook and other social Internet sites. They didn't take information found there as confirmation, however. Following Web leads, they contacted people who had posted and asked them what they knew. Parents of the victims were avoided out of compassion. Still, the journalists beat the by-then global competition by hours with what they learned. Major news organizations linked to videos, photographs and text on the social sites. After Bryce Carter posted a video shot from his dorm room to his LiveJournal page, he attracted international attention.

Facebook, MySpace and other sites popular with the young and tech savvy are increasingly fertile grounds for reporters—partly because those who wish to win over the young and tech savvy, including politicians and marketers, are putting potentially newsworthy information there. Presidential candidate John Edwards even listed his schedule on Twitter.com. More than 10 million professionals have registered at LinkedIn where they and you can find out who works where, with whom and when—and how to contact them. In all these sites, remember that the writers are not reporting for news organizations and that the material is raw. Check the information as you would that from any other source.

READING FOR BETTER WRITING

The best writers are voracious readers. That's because one of the best ways to improve your own writing is to critically read, analyze and dissect the writing of others. The Web allows you to access some of the best newspaper writing around easily—style section features in the *Washington Post,* trend stories in the *New York Times,* sports takeouts in the *Boston Globe*—to help your own writing.

And for pure writing and reporting inspiration, read the full-text originals of the latest Pulitzer Prize–winning work in every category from public service and spot news to editorial writing and criticism, starting with the 1995 winners. Go directly to the Pulitzer works at www.pulitzer.org.

CHAPTER 7

STRATEGIC SEARCHING

The last three chapters described specific Web sites that beat reporters can use in their daily reporting, but those represent just a tiny handful of the material available on the Internet. In this chapter we will explore how to find information on the Net when you do not have a specific Web address.

THINK STRATEGICALLY: DEVELOP A GAME PLAN

Commercial databases such as LexisNexis have spoiled some of us. Those well-designed, carefully thought out systems allow us to punch in a few keywords, swiftly expand or contract the scope of a search if needed, and within moments have the material we are seeking. Unfortunately, the Internet does not allow us that luxury. Instead of a single method of searching, there are dozens of search engines and directories that not only seek out information in different ways but look at different Internet materials and present the search results in different forms. That creates serious problems for reporters on deadline and makes searching the Internet a more complicated process than using a commercial database. That is why, before we start punching in keywords, we should develop a strategy for each search.

What Are You Looking For and Where Is It Likely to Be?

At the start of every search, ask yourself two questions: "What information am I looking for?" and "Which institutions will likely have that information?" The first question seems self-evident, but really isn't. Do we really know—specifically—what we are seeking? Let's say we are writing a piece on drug use on college campuses. What specific information do we want? At the beginning of the story, we would need to find statistics on drug use on campuses to quantify the issue and to show whether it is a growing or waning problem. We probably would want to get the specific drug policies of the colleges of interest to our audience. And we would want to find experts who could talk about the cultural phenomenon and historical dimensions of campus drug use. These are three areas where the Internet likely can be helpful in our reporting, but it is unlikely that the information will all be in

67

the same place. In effect, each question we have posed should be considered a distinct search. That is why it is so important to specify the information you are seeking.

Now that we have an idea of what we want, the next question we need to ask ourselves is, "Where would that information likely be?" At this point, we may simply not know, and will have to go straight to a search engine or Internet directory. But in many cases, time can be saved and results improved if we have some reasonable idea of where the information might be. In our campus drug example, the only credible sources of information for the drug statistics would be law enforcement agencies. We might start out with the FBI and work backward to the state police, then to the county, city, or campus police. For the drug policy of specific colleges, we would go directly to the logical sources—the colleges—and search within their Web sites for the written policies. And for the experts, we may either search again on the local university sites or on some of the expert databases discussed in Chapter 4.

Guessing

Now that we have figured out where the information is likely to be, we still need to find those specific Web sites. Again, before jumping on a search engine and typing in those key words, let's try something else first. Guess. That's right, just guess at the address. With the information from Chapter 2, we should be able to find many large Web sites without ever touching a search engine.

We know from Chapter 2 that the domain name—the basic Web address—usually has three main parts, separated by dots. The first is often (but not always) www, which of course stands for the World Wide Web. The second is a series of letters that gives the Web address its uniqueness. This often is either the full name of the institution or the institution's abbreviation. The last part of the main address is that three-letter suffix that tells us whether it is from the world of academia (.edu), government (.gov), commerce (.com) and so on (see p. 10). Let's try this out with our campus drug example. If we are looking for the Federal Bureau of Investigation, a good guess for that address might be www.fbi.gov (www for World Wide Web, fbi for Federal Bureau of Investigation, and .gov because it is a federal government site). If we are looking for the University of Maryland, we would try www.umd.edu (umd for University of Maryland and edu because it is an academic institution). In both cases, we would have saved ourselves the time of a search because those addresses are correct. Go back to Chapter 5 and look at how many of the addresses you probably could have guessed at correctly.

Does this mean you should spend lots of time guessing at an address? Certainly not, but try at least one or two addresses that you think would be logical, especially for relatively big institutions. It will save you precious minutes on deadline.

WHAT TO DO WHEN YOU
DON'T KNOW WHERE TO GO

The method of mapping out where information likely will be and then targeting that information is an efficient and effective way to get your hands on information quickly. But what if you don't have a clue about where to look? Let's try another example. Let's say we are about to launch into a news feature on racial diversity in U.S. newsrooms. We would want to first find statistics that both illustrate the racial inequities in the news workforce today and give a historical context. We would want to find any studies conducted about the impact of these inequities. We also would want to learn about efforts under way to correct the problem. And, ideally, we would like to get some expert sources who could speak authoritatively about the subject. But, unlike with the campus drug story, we really don't know where to turn. For this story, we will have to search the Internet using one of two tools: directories or search engines.

DIRECTORIES

Internet directories are straightforward hierarchical systems that group Web sites into categories and subcategories. To search for information, we would go from a very general group into more specific subgroups until we have reached the type of information sought (called "drilling down").

Directories, which are assembled by editors, are excellent for casual users interested in broad, general topic areas. Reporters may want to try directories at the beginning of a big enterprise story on an unfamiliar topic but not when looking for specifics. The most popular directory is maintained at the Yahoo! site (see below).

SEARCH ENGINES

Here's the lead on Internet search engines: There are many, they all search for different things, they all search in different ways and they all produce different results. And the kicker? You can do the same search on every engine available and still not know if what you are looking for is somewhere on the Internet.

How Search Engines Work

To understand how to use search engines, we need to know a bit about how they work and why they are imperfect. Search engines are Web sites designed to help you find information on the Internet. Each search site works by compiling a database of information on Web sites. The search engine's database is compiled by robot programs that wander around the Web looking for sites to include in the engine's database. But each engine produces different—in many cases extraordinarily different—results on the same keyword search because of the differences in both what information is collected for the database and how that information is analyzed by the program. Some retrieve only the titles of Web pages (the brief description located above the toolbar in your software program), some record parts of the document and others index the entire page.

Another problem is that there is no standard search method among the various engines. Some use upper- and lowercases, others don't; some recognize articles, others do not. Not even all of the search engines use common Boolean connectors such as AND, NOT, and OR. What search engines do have in common is an attempt to present results of a search in order of importance, with the top results, or "hits," from a search representing the best matches to that particular search. It is like the computer equivalent of the inverted pyramid. But, of course, each search engine has its own idea of what is an ideal match. Some weigh the number of times the keywords are mentioned in a site. Others give value to *where* those keywords are mentioned in the document, giving more weight to keywords toward the top of a site.

How to Use Search Engines Effectively

Your search will depend in large part on the search engine you have selected. But there are some basic concepts that should be implemented in all of your reporting searches.

Take Advantage of Basic Commands to Tailor a Search. Each search engine uses its own set of commands to narrow a search by combining words and phrases that are likely to appear in the document. Searching multiple sets of words and phrases makes your search much more specific. You can find the individual commands under a section called "tips," "help," or "search tips" on the main page of each engine.

Be Specific in Keyword Selection. Select specific search words and phrases over more general words and phrases (as long as you are confident the selected keywords are likely to appear in the sought-after documents). The goal should be to come up with keywords that are most likely to appear in the documents being sought while unlikely to appear in unrelated sites.

Be Precise in Keyword Selection. Search engines, like everything in the computer world, take things quite literally. For instance, the former managing editor of *The New York Times,* Eugene Roberts, is called Gene by many. But he often is referred to in print by his full first name. So a search of Roberts should include both the phrases "Gene Roberts" and "Eugene Roberts."

Review Results Top to Bottom. Most search engines display search results in some type of hierarchical order—from what they believe to be the best fits to your search query to the least likely fits. Therefore, that is how you should always review the search results—from top to bottom—paying much more attention to the first page or two of results.

Analyze the Addresses of Results. Once search results are returned, do not just start opening up the Web pages. First take a moment to analyze not only the brief description of the site, but, just as importantly, look at the Internet address. Is it a government, educational, commercial, or other kind of site? Can you tell if it is from a group that you know? A few moments spent looking at the Web addresses and descriptions can save precious minutes used in waiting to connect to the various sites.

The Major Search Engines

There are lots of different search engines out there, all with their pluses and minuses. Let's take a quick look at some of the most popular engines.

Google. The authors' (current) favorite for its comprehensiveness and clarity. Go directly to the advanced search functions at

www.google.com/advanced_search?hl=en

Scroll down on the page and note the link for searching all U.S. federal, state and local government sites. From the home page you can search video, maps, images, news. In the pull-down menu, link to searches for blogs, books, groups and more. See the help page for a rundown of the many other options at

www.google.com/support/

Yahoo! Since 2002, Yahoo! has used a search engine (a crawler) for its main searches but retained its original directory (sites chosen by humans) service as well. When "category" links appear on a search results page they lead to the directory database. The "combination" search is from the home page at

http://search.yahoo.com/

For a directory-only search use

http://dir.yahoo.com/

Microsoft Live Search. The search service used to be known as MSN Search. It went from using live editors to Yahoo! listings. When Microsoft developed its crawler, the name changed. It's also known as Windows Live.

www.live.com/

AltaVista. A previous favorite. Advanced searching abilities make AltaVista among the most powerful search engines for reporters. It's currently supplied with Yahoo!'s database.

www.altavista.com/web/adv

FIGURE 7.1   An IceRocket tag cloud shows search words and relative popularity.

(Reprinted with permission of PR Newswire Association LLC.)

Ask.com. Used to be Ask Jeeves. Although it became famous for encouraging users to pose queries in the form of traditional questions that were answered from human-derived data, Ask uses crawler technology.

www.ask.com

Lycos. The results are supplied by Ask.com. The home page is a portal that offers quick access to top hits on YouTube, MySpace and Google video, lists the top 50 Lycos searches, etc.

www.lycos.com/

Icerocket. Searches blogs or finds them through "tag" searches. A visual device, called a tag cloud, displays the words used in searches and indicates how popular they are by the word's relative size. You click on the word to initiate the search. Also offers MySpace searches. (See Figure 7.1.)

www.icerocket.com

Some search sites offer access to more than one search engine. These include MetaCrawler (www.metacrawler.com) and DogPile (www.dogpile .com). Northern Light (www.nlresearch.com/pubsearch.php) specializes in business research and lets you browse topics and search journals. Twingine (http://twingine.com) and DoubleTrust (http://www.doubletrust.net) do Google and Yahoo simultaneously and compare the differences.

Most Internet-savvy reporters have their favorite search tools. But the effectiveness of your searching is much more dependent on knowing the various advanced search functions of a specific engine, as opposed to which tool you select. Pick a search engine and make yourself an expert in that tool's various functions. If you need a bit of fun while searching, check out Ms. Dewey at

www.msdewey.com

Search Services

Notification

Google alerts sends daily customized search results via e-mail.

www.google.com/alerts

Mobile info

Set up a Google menu on your phone: www.google.com/mobile/ Text message Google at 466453 with SMS (Short Message Service) queries and get the answer sent to your mobile device. Send maps to your phone.

Yahoo One Search. To try it, type m.yahoo.com into your browser. For more information: http://mobile.yahoo.com/?refer=1OFADX

AGGREGATORS OR READERS

A huge breakthrough in the way Web content is created resulted in the ability to display one piece of information in more than one format. The same headline, for example, can be shown on a Web page, sent to your cell phone and tracked by an automated search program thanks to XML coding. This is what aggregators, also known as news readers, look for. RSS (Really Simple Syndication) and Atom feeds are examples of XML material.

Once you subscribe to a reader and tell it what to look for, spiders crawl the Web in search of current material that can be "pulled" into a common Web page for you to see. Many kinds of content can be collected, including blogs, vlogs, podcasts, news stories and video. If you want to watch many feeds, look for an aggregator that lets you use keywords to focus (or filter) the search for fewer and better results. These are a few of the most popular:

Google Reader   www.google.com/reader/view/

Bloglines   www.bloglines.com

Newsgator. Free online RSS reader (other services are sold).

www.newsgator.com or www.newsgator.com/ngs/order1.aspx

Awasu. Free basic service for blogs and news channels.

www.awasu.com

STORAGE AND RETRIEVAL

Sure, you can use your browser's bookmark tool—but that means you have to use that browser on that computer each time you want to see what you've saved. If you work at different computers and use different browsers, you'll have some bookmarks here, some there. There are free services that go far beyond basic bookmarking and allow unified files. One of the current best is Furl, which bills itself as a personal Web file. You can save up to 5 gigabytes of Web pages into an archive that can be organized by keyword, tag and topic and retrieved and searched from any computer anywhere. The handy "Furl It" button (called a bookmarklet) works in AOL, IE, Firefox, Mozilla, Opera and Safari.

www.furl.net/home.jsp

Other bookmarkers include:

> *OnlyWire.* Use multiple services? This one will feed them all. No storage.
>   http://onlywire.com/
>
> *Del.icio.us.* One of the most popular social networks, it's a free site de-signed for storing and sharing links to Web pages.
>   http://del.icio.us/about/
>
> *Times File.* Not just for *New York Times* stories. The basic service is free.
>   http://timesfile.nytimes.com/view.jsp

FIND WHAT'S POPULAR

> *Newsvine.com.* User-submitted news sorted into topical areas. Can be customized to show news of specific regions. You get space for a col-umn and a "Seed Newsvine" tool to easily contribute articles.
>
>   www.newsvine.com/
>
> *PopURLS:* Popular links to the latest Web buzz.
>
>   http://popurls.com/
>
> *Reddit.com.* There's more of a game atmosphere at this site for user-submitted links. Readers rate what they like or dislike, comment, earn karma points. You can store preferences.
>
>   http://reddit.com/help/

HOW MANY SEARCHES?

How many searches should you conduct on how many different search en-gines? There is no easy answer, but remember that you are using the Internet in part to *save* yourself reporting time. It is easy to get so caught up in trying to find the information on various search engines that you wind up wasting too much time. We recommend that, for deadline reporting, first think about the best search terms and then conduct that search on one or two search engines (or search options as with Google Scholar and Google advanced search), tak-ing advantage of the specific search commands for those engines. After that there are diminishing returns, as you see from the previous examples.

Now that we have some search strategies to go with our knowledge of the Web and our specific Web sites, let's put it all together in developing an electronic beat system.

CHAPTER 8

BUILDING AN ELECTRONIC BEAT

The first few hours and days on a new beat, or in a new newsroom, are spent quickly getting up to speed on the issues and players to be covered. The first stop is getting briefed by veteran editors, reporters and, when possible, the person whose beat you are taking over. Next is thumbing through recent clips. Then, time permitting, you might go out and introduce yourself to new sources, perhaps collecting background information, documents, and directories along the way. The idea is to familiarize yourself quickly with the territory and gather sources and resources that can be accessed quickly on deadline. And, ideally, you will have a chance to do all of this *before* you have to begin filing daily stories.

We should take this same approach in creating an Internet beat system—gathering, organizing and familiarizing ourselves with potentially useful sources of information while *not* on deadline. With an electronic beat system already in place, we then can jump on the Internet with confidence to access information quickly and effectively on deadline.

We will find beat-specific Internet sites by tapping into the search skills from the previous chapter in addition to the source lists of Chapters 4, 5 and 6. Each site should be examined to find out where the useful information is located. And we will organize these beat sites by using bookmarks so these sources can be quickly accessed under deadline pressure.

TYPES OF BEATS

Beats can be broken down into three basic categories—geographic-based beats (the Washington County reporter), issue-oriented beats (the environmental reporter) and beats that cover institutions (the City Hall reporter). All reporters fall into one of those three categories, even general assignment reporters (the circulation area that their publications cover is a geographic beat). Let's look at how we can find and organize Internet sources for each of these three beat types.

THE GEOGRAPHIC BEAT

Desktop Reporting Tools. The basic reporting tools discussed in Chapter 4—Web phone directories, mapping programs, expert source databases, the Census Bureau Statistical Abstract, the customizable Freedom of Information Act and state public records law templates and the state open meeting and public records law—all should be bookmarked. These tools will be the same whether the beat is geographic-, issue- or institution-based.

Daily News. Use *AJR* NewsSources (p. 62, www.ajr.org) to find the appropriate local and regional daily newspapers. You also may want to include major national publications such as *The New York Times* for potential story ideas that can be localized.

Demographic Data. Bookmark not only the main Census Bureau Web page (p. 41, www.census.gov) but click down and bookmark the census pages for new press releases and customizable census databases for your town or county. Also locate your state data center via the Census Bureau, explore that site and bookmark the useful sections. Demographic data is especially important if a reporter is new to the area.

State Government. Locate your state's main Web site via GlobalComputing (p. 60, www.globalcomputing.com/states.html) and bookmark it. You also may want to find and bookmark some key pages, such as an employees' directory and the state government manual.

State Legislature. Bookmark the state Legislature home page and the pages of your local state lawmakers.

Local Government. Find your town, city and/or county government either through the state Web site or via one of the search engines or directories discussed in the previous chapter. Spend some time learning what is available on the sites. Bookmark the home page plus useful pages inside.

Schools. Using a Web directory or search engine, locate and bookmark Web sites for both the local school systems and area colleges and universities.

Major Employers. Find, evaluate and bookmark the company Web sites for each of the major employers and public utilities in your coverage area by using the methods in Chapter 7. Then go to the Securities and Exchange Commission, the Occupational Safety and Health Administration, and FECInfo sites (listed in Chapter 5) and bookmark the data pages for those companies.

Special Interest Groups. Employ search engines to find the local special-interest groups in your area, including lobbying groups, nonprofit organizations and associations, unions, business groups, community and civic organizations and churches. Then, traveling down from the main state Web page, find and bookmark the secretary of state's page on corporate and nonprofit filings.

Local Politics. Using either the Republican (www.rnc.org) and Democratic (www.democrats.org) national Web sites (p. 50) or search engines, find and save the locations for the state parties, county parties and local politicians. This is useful not only to access information for stories, but to monitor how politicians and political parties are communicating with their constituencies and what they are saying.

Courts. Check through the state government home page to search for state appellate courts online. Then bookmark the appropriate U.S. District Court, U.S. Bankruptcy Court, U.S. Circuit Court, the U.S. Supreme Court and other legal resources from Chapter 5 (p. 54).

Federal Register. Go to the Federal Register (p. 42) and bookmark it to conduct regular searches for federal government actions and proposals affecting the town, city or county you are covering.

Search Engines. Bookmark your favorite search engines for quick access.

THE ISSUE BEAT

The Web sites for desktop reporting tools, daily news and search engines are the same as those listed previously for the locale-based beat. But there are some substantial differences.

State Government. In addition to the general state government Web page, drill down to locate and analyze the state agencies that regulate your issue. Bookmark not only the main agency page but also inside pages that may be particularly valuable in your reporting.

State Legislature. Bookmark the main state Legislature page and committees dealing with your subject area.

Local Government. Save the main page and the local government agencies that affect your issue.

Special-Interest Groups. Find the local, state and national special interest groups that are players on your issue beat, including lobbying groups, business associations, unions and other organizations.

Federal Agencies. Find the federal agencies dealing with your issue, surf those sites and bookmark the main pages and useful inside pages.

Specialty Publications. Employing either search engines or MediaFinder (p. 65, www.mediafinder.com), locate and bookmark the specialty newsletters and magazines that follow your issue.

■ ■ ■ ■ ■

BOX 8.1

Frank Sweeney explains how the Internet helped the San Jose Mercury News *cover devastating California floods.*

Our coverage of the floods of 1997 had a high-tech edge.

Some reporters made extensive use of the National Weather Service's home page from Monterey (www.nws.mbay.net), in particular its link to the river and rainfall page, where there are links to river flow reporting stations.

We could see, hour by hour, how high the water was rising on the big rivers of the Central Valley and how much was flowing into and out of the major reservoirs. For some rivers, there were graphs showing the rise and fall of the water compared to the flood-stage level.

The California Data Exchange Center home page (cdec.water.CA.gov) has links to hundreds of gauges and sensors that measure river flow, rainfall and temperatures. This page even offered aerial photos of flooded areas and maps of levee breaks.

Journalism Organizations. Check Chapter 12 to see if there are any journalism organizations that specialize in your beat area. These can provide various resources and indicate other good sources.

Beat Organizers. Some Internet-savvy journalists have shared their own electronic beat systems with fellow reporters on the Web and journalism organizations. One of the best is the issue-categorized Beat Source Guide created by IRE-Investigative Reporters and Editors and available at www.ire.org/resourcecenter/initial-search-beat.html.

You undoubtedly will find Web resources on these pages that we have yet to come across. But we strongly recommend that you look at these reporter sites only *after* you have done the searches on your own. The power of creating a beat-oriented list of resources is that it is tailored specifically to you and your publication. That cannot be reproduced en masse.

THE INSTITUTION BEAT

The institution-based beat is analogous to the issue beat. The same categories can be applied.

So far in this book we have looked at the World Wide Web portion of the Internet. In the next three chapters, we will look at some other Internet tools that can help reporters and editors, beginning with e-mail.

■　■　■　■　■

BOX 8.2

Heather Newman of the Detroit Free Press *tapped the power of the Internet for an in-depth look at standardized tests for Michigan elementary schools.*

We did a major project early in 1998 looking at our state standardized tests for elementary schools in Michigan. The project never would have been possible without computers, and would not have been as complete or as timely without the Internet. The thrust of our project was this: Educators had been telling us that school test scores could be dramatically affected by factors outside of schools' control, such as poverty or the education of the parents. Yet standardized tests in Michigan are used for everything from custody battles to real estate listings, and the state accreditation formula, which affects how schools are funded, depends almost entirely on one set of tests: the Michigan Educational Assessment Program, or MEAP scores.

　　We set out to determine what, if any, effect factors outside of districts' control had on test scores and whether those scores were being used wisely. It was a six-month project, scheduled between daily and shorter efforts. We started by sending out a request to ProfNet (profnet@profnet.com) for experts who could help us, and searching their expert database (www.profnet.com) to see whether we could turn up any names there. We got more than three dozen responses, all educational statisticians who could help us structure our analysis.

　　Next, we turned to the Net for Web sites that had information about standardized testings, which eventually turned into a sidebar for the main piece. This directed us toward more experts we could consult and additional factors we could consider when analyzing the tests. We also used Lexis-Nexis to hunt for packages written by other newspapers and magazines that might mirror what we were trying to do.

　　Once we had a list of factors that might affect test scores, given to us by our experts and our research, we set out to find that data on a district or school level for Michigan. All the data the state education office kept, including many of the factors we needed, was on their Web site in searchable or downloadable form. We also discovered, through the Web, two CD-ROMs produced by the U.S. Department of Education and the National Center for Education Statistics (the School District Data Book [SDDB] and the Common Core of Data), which included yet more information about districts and schools across the state. We ordered both these discs (one is free; the other costs $15). When technical problems arose with the SDDB, we contacted the person who handled tech support for the program via e-mail, and he e-mailed the solutions back to us and attached some files we needed to his correspondence.

　　We combined all these databases into one huge data set that included hundreds of bits of information on each of Michigan's 500-plus school districts. Then we set about doing our analysis, based on the advice we had gotten from our experts and some standard statistics techniques. We found that, in urban and surburban areas, factors beyond a district's control accounted for the majority of differences between districts' scores, which meant that what was happening inside the classroom had less effect than what was happening at home. We e-mailed the results of our study and the supporting computer files to a few statisticians, who reviewed our work for us to make sure we had dotted our *i*'s and crossed our *t*'s.

We conducted many of our interviews via e-mail, and set up quite a few of the ones we conducted in person using e-mail messages. Without the Internet, the project would not have had nearly the depth it did, nor would it have been as successful.

CHAPTER 9

ELECTRONIC MAIL

Years ago, Bill Loving, the former computer-assisted reporting editor at the Minneapolis *Star Tribune*, now at the *Los Angeles Times*, said that electronic mail is "replacing the fax as the communication tool of choice." He was right. E-mail is faster than faxes, usually arriving in a matter of moments, while faxes often get caught up on busy phone lines, jammed and backed-up fax machines or machines out of paper. E-mail is cheaper than faxes, costing only the monthly Internet connection fees in contrast to the long-distance telephone charges and paper for fax machines. E-mail is more reliable than faxes, landing directly in a person's electronic mail system instead of arriving on a fax machine probably shared by an entire office. And e-mail holds more potential as an innovative reporting tool.

E-MAIL AS A REPORTING TOOL

Below are some of the advantages of incorporating e-mail into your life as a working journalist.

> *Routine Deadline Reporting Questions.* If you need to find out a relatively simple piece of information from a source, such as getting a single fact confirmed, an e-mail can help circumvent those dreaded late afternoon games of phone tag that turn reporters prematurely gray. E-mail often will get returned more quickly than the phone message because it is faster and easier for the source. You would not want to conduct in-depth interviews via e-mail, but for the perfunctory question, it can be a valuable time-saver.

> *Contacting Hard-to-Reach Sources.* Sometimes e-mail is the best, or perhaps only way, to contact a source. Phineas Fiske, when an editorial writer at *Newsday*, tells the story of his efforts to track down a former state official who was traveling in Russia and could not be reached. Fiske, knowing the former official traveled with a laptop computer, sent a message to his e-mail address. The source responded within hours.

Contacting Reluctant Sources. We all have experienced the source who is integral to the story, but ducks us at every turn and refuses to return phone messages. Or perhaps you cannot even get past roadblocks set up by overprotective secretaries or paranoid public relations officers. E-mail is another way to make direct contact, allowing you to make your case about why the source should agree to an interview. And, unlike traditional mail and even phone messages, e-mail usually goes directly to the person, not through a secretary, assistant, or flak.

Contacting Webmasters. By now you are probably familiar with the e-mail addresses for "webmasters"—the techies who run the Web sites—located at the bottom of most home pages. Neill A. Borowski, former director of computer-assisted reporting and analysis at the *Philadelphia Inquirer,* suggests writing to webmasters when looking for data that is not available on the Web pages, but may exist somewhere within the agency that runs the Web site. Borowski e-mailed the webmaster of the New Jersey State Data Center requesting housing data from the 1970 and 1980 census for particular New Jersey towns. He received the data within a day.

Contacting Multiple Sources Quickly. E-mail also is a fast and efficient way to contact numerous sources on the same subject. For instance, in the preparation of this book, Callahan wanted to contact journalists who he thought were some of the best in Internet reporting and ask them to contribute a piece. It would have taken days to reach each journalist by telephone, but the e-mail connections took just a few moments.

Keeping in Touch with Sources. E-mail also is a good way to keep in contact with sources. After his series on toxins in fertilizer (p. 4), Duff Wilson of the *Seattle Times* sent the story and follow-ups to more than 50 sources, asking for their comments. He reported getting leads on several follow-up stories from the e-mail contacts.

Exchanging Ideas with Colleagues. Among the wonderful things about journalism are the professional bonds and friendships formed among colleagues. Some of our best friends—and people we respect most professionally—are the journalists we worked with at our college newspapers and our first jobs out of school. But, of course, most of those folks are now scattered across the country. E-mail provides a way to stay connected with those people and to exchange ideas and concerns about stories and other journalism issues. It can be quite helpful to have a trusted colleague read a draft of a big enterprise package before sending it off to your editor. The more input you have on a piece of journalism from colleagues whom you trust and respect, the better the finished product will be.

Connection to Readers. Some publications include reporters' e-mail addresses at the end of stories so that readers can contact them directly. This has limited use. Certainly hearing reader feedback to stories is important, but such unsolicited comments often come from the extreme ends of a given issue. Furthermore, people connected to e-mail still do not represent a socioeconomic cross section of the country.

Over the Transom Sources. E-mail also provides another outlet for new sources to provide tips, but again caution should be exercised. Never assume that people who contact you via e-mail are actually who they say they are. Always check it out.

Electronic Releases and Updates. Most agencies, corporations, and special-interest groups send regular alerts and press releases to interested reporters via e-mail instead of fax (see p. 90).

DECODING E-MAIL ADDRESSES

There are several ways to find e-mail addresses. The best for journalists (because it is the fastest) is making an educated guess, in much the same way we guessed at Web addresses in Chapter 7. But in order to make a good guess, we need to decipher e-mail addresses.

Computer Host Addresses. E-mail addresses have two main parts, divided by an "at" sign (@). The part after the @ symbol is the address of the computer that is hosting the e-mail user. These host addresses are similar to the home page addresses of Web pages. They have two or more parts separated by dots. Reading from right to left, the parts of the host computer address go from the most general to the most specific. The section farthest to the right uses the same three-letter suffixes as we saw in the Web addresses in Chapter 3 (.com = commercial sites, .gov = government sites, .edu = education sites and so on). Let's use an example. Let's say John Smith works for the *Seattle Gazette.* His e-mail address at work is

jsmith@seattlegazette.com

In this case, "seattlegazette.com" is the computer address. Reading from right to left, "com" stands for a commercial organization. Next comes an abbreviation for the institution of the host computer, in this case "seattlegazette" for the newspaper. From this analysis we can deduce that *Seattle Gazette* employees have e-mail addresses that end "@seattlegazette.com." All e-mail addresses can be analyzed in the same way.

User Identifications. Now let's tackle the first part of the e-mail address, known as the user ID. Because e-mail systems are developed in large part so people within the same organization can communicate easily with each other, computer system designers usually create user-ID systems that are uniform. This avoids the problem of having to memorize or look up e-mail addresses each time you want to send an electronic message. Common user-ID systems include the first and last name, the last name then the first name, the first initial of the first name and the full last name, the last name then the first initial of the first name, just the last name and just a specified number of letters from the last name. Looking at our examples, we can tell from John Smith's address (jsmith) that the *Seattle Gazette* user-ID system is the first initial of the first name and the full last name. That means we now know the precise e-mail for virtually everyone who works at the *Seattle Gazette.*

FINDING E-MAIL ADDRESSES

Guessing. Now that we know how to analyze electronic mail system addresses, we can guess at the e-mail addresses of sources once we have the address for at least one other person in that organization. This can be a powerful tool in your reporting. For instance, most public relations officers would give you their e-mail addresses, but might be reluctant to hand out the addresses of the agency head or other potential news sources in the organization. Armed only with the PR officer's e-mail address, you probably can deduce the addresses for everyone else there.

Institutional Directories. What if you do not have any e-mail addresses at an institution? Then you should find the institution's Web site and search for a directory of addresses.

General E-Mail Directories. What if the institution does not have an e-mail directory or if the person you are looking for is not part of a large institution? In those cases, go to one of a variety of electronic mail search engines. The search engines are similar to the programs that look for Web sites discussed in Chapter 7. They are found on both the telephone directories discussed in Chapter 4 and on the major search engines.

NEWSROOM POLICIES
ON E-MAIL COMMUNICATION

The Associated Press has some specific guidelines for the use of e-mail in reporting. They include:

- Represent the organization. An e-mail with a reporter's affiliation attached is similar to that reporter appearing at a public meeting or writing a letter on company letterhead.
- Avoid political activity. "AP has long-standing rules against News employees participating in political activities or taking sides on matters of public debate," the policy states. "These rules apply to electronic communication as well."
- Follow the etiquette of e-mail (such as not typing in all capital letters, which can be perceived by recipients as *shouting* electronically).
- Check all e-mail sources of information. Remember that e-mail addresses can be faked.

PROFNET

We talked about the ProfNet database of expert sources back in Chapter 4, but ProfNet is best known to reporters as an e-mail system for finding expert sources. ProfNet will take a reporter's e-mail request for a particular type of expert source and distribute it to public relations offices in about 7,000 institutions worldwide, including 1,200 universities, 4,000 corporations, 1,200 PR firms, 1,000 nonprofit organizations and government agencies and 100 think tanks, scientific associations and labs. Reporter requests are sent out three times a day (10:30 A.M., 1:30 P.M. and 4 P.M. Eastern time) to the 14,000 participating public relations officials. It is the same idea as calling your local

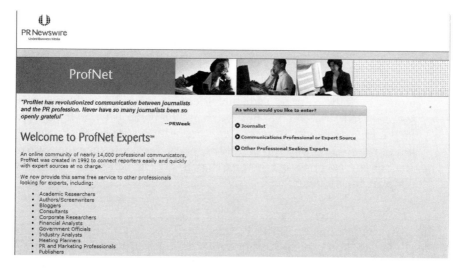

FIGURE 9.1   Home page of ProfNet at http://profnet.prnewswire.com

university for an expert source, but, instead of making one phone call, you are making 7,000 simultaneously.

ProfNet has grown dramatically since it was started by Daniel Forbush at the State University of New York at Stony Brook in 1992. It is a subsidiary of PR NewsWire and more than 20,000 reporters now actively use the site.

To use ProfNet, send an e-mail query to profnet@profnet.com or register at https://profnet.prnewswire.com.

Some keys to a ProfNet search include:

Deadlines. ProfNet is designed for enterprise stories, not spot news coverage. Also, make sure to include a deadline in your message (the "deadline" should be when you need to hear from the source, not when the story is actually due to your editor).

Specificity. You are not looking for dozens of potential sources; you are seeking the small handful of truly expert sources for your story. The best ProfNet requests are the ones that have a great deal of specificity.

Audience. Think about what types of institutions should receive your request. If you want your request to go only to universities and think tanks, for instance, make that clear in your query.

Identification. Make it clear whom you represent and describe your news organization in terms of type of publication, audience and circulation.

Response. Specify how you want to be contacted (e-mail, phone or fax).

Confidentiality. ProfNet searches are supposed to be confidential, but if you are working on a particularly sensitive story be sure to write your query in a way that does not tip off the story. You also can cloak your identity (but if you are sitting on the next Watergate, probably best to skip ProfNet altogether).

Verification. And, of course, once you have gotten the names and numbers of some sources, do not just assume they are truly expert on your topic. Check them out by asking the PR officials to provide the potential sources' credentials on the subject at hand. Or better yet, find the experts on the Web and check out their background yourself. Just because you found the sources through a ProfNet query does not make the sources any better (or worse) on their face than if you had called the university, nonprofit or think tank.

The only difference—and it's a big one—is that you have widened your search enormously. As the *Washington Post*'s Boyce Rensberger said about ProfNet: "You can catch sources that you never would have thought to go after. It's the difference between fishing with a hook and fishing with a net."

■ ■ ■ ■ ■

BOX 9.1

Excerpts from Bill Dedman's Power Reporting Web site at PowerReporting.com

NATIONAL CRIMINAL JUSTICE REFERENCE SERVICE

www.ncjrs.gov/

A deep resource of information on criminal justice: corrections, courts, crime prevention, statistics, drugs, juveniles, law enforcement, research, victims. Maintains several mailing lists about police work. Some lists are open, and others are restricted to law officers. Topics include bike cops, cop fleet, high tech crime fighting, criminal justice, emergency management, Department of Justice announcements, law enforcement analysts, firearms instructors and public safety communications.

U.S. BUREAU OF THE CENSUS

www.census.gov/mp/www/subscribe.html

If you're on the Census mailing lists, you hear about upcoming data releases in population and economics, so you can localize a national story or nationalize a local one. If you're not on the list, you're out of luck. Subscribe to one of four lists: the monthly product announcement, the biweekly bulletin, a monthly list of feature ideas and the press releases (including info on new data).

U.S. GENERAL ACCOUNTABILITY OFFICE

www.gao.gov

Previously known as the General Accounting Office. A lot of journalists use this one. The GAO Daybook is a daily update on reports, documents and testimony. It comes in two forms: an announcement by title and number of pages; and, a few days later, with a URL to the GAO site.

SUPREME COURT BULLETINS FROM CORNELL

www.law.cornell.edu/focus/bulletins.html

U.S. Supreme Court opinions are distributed, in syllabus form, by Cornell University's Legal Information Institute within hours of their release. Also has decisions from the New York Court of Appeals.

U.S. CONSUMER PRODUCT SAFETY COMMISSION

www.cpsc.gov/cpsclist.asp

You can automatically get product recall notices from the Consumer Product Safety Commission.

U.S. DEPARTMENT OF AGRICULTURE ALERTS

http://usda.mannlib.cornell.edu/MannUsda/aboutEmailService.do

Everything from chickens to cranberries. The Ag Department has 70 e-mail information services, including information on imports, exports, prices, chemicals, milk and walnuts.

U.S. ENVIRONMENTAL PROTECTION AGENCY

https://lists.epa.gov/read/all_forums

More than 70 EPA mailing lists on a range of topics.

U.S. FEDERAL COMMUNICATIONS COMMISSION

www.fcc.gov/Daily_Releases/Daily_Digest/1999/

The FCC Daily Digest provides a synopsis of Commission orders, news releases, speeches and titles of public notices. The Digest is published every business afternoon. A searchable archive is on the Web site.

U.S. FOOD AND DRUG ADMINISTRATION

www.fda.gov/

The FDA sends out safety alerts, public health advisories and other FDA safety notices. To subscribe, send mail to fdalists@www.fda.gov with the text, "subscribe dev-alert."

FED MAILING LISTS

http://research.stlouisfed.org/fred2/

Subscribe to Federal Reserve Economic Data series and publications on national and international economic trends. (Original FRED database replaced July 2007.)

WHITE HOUSE BRIEFING ROOM

www.whitehouse.gov

White House press releases and briefings. To subscribe to White House press releases, call the White House Press Office, (202) 456-2580.

10K WIZARD FULL-TEXT SEARCH OF SEC DOCUMENTS

www.10kwizard.com

No longer free. Allows full-text searching of public documents filed by public companies (companies with shareholders) in the U.S. Search filings by public companies and even receive e-mail alerts when a certain word or phrase shows up in a filing. Allows easy sorting of results by date or company. Note that the default search is the past 12 months; can be changed to go back several years. Download tables in Excel format.

CENTER FOR RESPONSIVE POLITICS

www.opensecrets.org

Political junkies and anyone looking into a regulatory issue will appreciate the alerts from the Center for Responsive Politics, a nonprofit with searchable databases of U.S. campaign contributions. It's easy to look up campaign contributions here, with the usual limitation that there is a time lag between the contributions and reporting by the Federal Election Commission. Staff at CRP have the most useful publications and advice on covering campaign finance and will provide data in a hurry, sliced the way you want, for a small fee.

EUREKALERT!

www.eurekalert.org

EurekAlert! is produced by the American Association for the Advancement of Science (AAAS). It offers daily e-mail notices for reporters and editors only. One is a list of scientific research papers; you have to agree to honor the embargo.

NATIONAL SCIENCE FOUNDATION

www.nsf.gov/mynsf/

NSF offers an e-mail alert of all new publications, or only those matching your interests, or will make a custom Web page for you. Plenty of information on science and mathematics, including curriculum development.

U.S. CENTERS FOR DISEASE CONTROL
MAILING LISTS

www.cdc.gov/subscribe.html

The CDC offers 19 mailing lists on infectious diseases, HIV/AIDS, morbidity and mortality, minority health and national health surveys.

BUSINESS INFORMATION SERVICE

www.bisnis.doc.gov/bisnis/new_bisnis.cfm

Focus on Newly Independent States, from the U.S. Department of Commerce: biweekly e-mail reports with trade leads, investment leads, conference announcements and general information. Also industry and country reports.

DEFENSE SYSTEMS DAILY

http://defense-data.com/Headlines/mailing_list.cgi

Defense and aerospace headlines every day from this British publisher.

ECONDATA

http://econdata.net/

Links to more than 300 sources of local and regional socioeconomic data in the U.S. A valuable resource for finding regional, state and local economic and marketing data on income, employment, housing starts and other economic statistics for states, cities, counties and regions across the nation. Site includes a User's Guide to Socioeconomic Data for Understanding Your Regional Economy, a 100-page "complete dummies" style guide to finding and using data. Developed by Joe Cortright and Andrew Reamer and sponsored in part by the U.S. Economic Development Administration. Also offers an e-mail alert for registered users.

EDGAR ONLINE

> www.edgar-online.com

Filings by public companies to the U.S. Securities and Exchange Commission. Will send e-mail when new forms are filed by companies you specify. Allows searches by executive's name.

FEDERAL CONSUMER INFORMATION CENTER

> www.pueblo.gsa.gov/

Visitors can read, print out or download the text of more than 200 federal publications on topics such as cars, money, children, education, home, travel, small business, food and health. The site features all of the publications listed in the current Consumer Information Catalog and others that are not included in the catalog, or that were featured in previous editions of the catalog. The site also features a consumer help section, listings of current scams and recalls, links to hundreds of government, corporate, nonprofit and other helpful web sites and the latest news from federal agencies. The site also has a page where the media can sign up for regular FCIC alerts.

ELECTRONIC PRESS RELEASES AND NEWS ALERTS

More government agencies, companies and special-interest groups are making press releases and other news alerts available via e-mail. The automated systems are similar to the mailing lists described in the next chapter. Reporters electronically subscribe to a particular list and they automatically receive that organization's releases. The e-mail press release has several advantages over the traditional fax. It is faster, it is more reliable (e-mail comes directly to the recipient's account, while faxes are usually shared by an entire newsroom or section of the newsroom and can get lost), and it is cheaper (it saves on fax paper).

Bill Dedman, the Pulitzer prize–winning reporter of the *Atlanta Journal-Constitution*, now in Chicago writing for *The New York Times,* has done extensive research on the proliferation of e-mail news alerts. The information in Box 9.1 is excerpted from his Web site. The full site is available at www.PowerReporting.com/category/alerts_for_journalists.

E-MAIL AS NEWS

In some states, e-mail transmissions written by public officials are considered open records. Statutes and case law vary on this question, but it can be a treasure trove of news stories for investigative reporters. Look at the public records law in your state (p. 38) to find out whether e-mail transmissions by public officials are considered public records.

CHAPTER 10

DISCUSSION GROUPS: E-MAIL LISTS AND NEWSGROUPS

The previous chapter discussed how to use electronic mail on a one-to-one (or one-to-few) basis and how to receive news releases and alerts. But the Internet also allows users to quickly send e-mail to special-interest groups. There are more than 100,000 of these "mailing lists," discussion groups on specific topics that allow a user to send a single message to one site and have that message distributed automatically and simultaneously to everyone who has subscribed to that particular list. Users then can respond to the entire membership of the list simply by responding to the list address. Subject areas range from everything from botany to Bob Dylan. Most mailing lists are "open," or "public," meaning anyone can subscribe. Some are "closed," or "private," which means you have to obtain permission from the list manager to subscribe. Most lists are unmoderated, but some have moderators who filter the content that goes out. Nearly all the lists are free.

The e-mail-based mailing lists, or discussion groups, are often referred to generically as "listservs." But Listserv is actually the corporate name for just one type of mailing list, and Listserv lists make up only a portion of all Internet mailing lists. Listproc and Majordomo are two other popular mailing list services.

Newsgroups—which, contrary to their name, are not necessarily dedicated to discussing news—are similar to mailing lists: They provide a place where people on the Internet with similar interests gather and discuss specific issues. And like mailing lists, newsgroups can be useful to journalists "listening in" to special-interest groups, seeking out sources or asking questions of a particular group.

But mailing lists and newsgroups operate differently—something like the difference between a magazine subscription and a bulletin board. Lists, like magazine subscriptions, automatically provide you with all of the information being circulated as soon as you subscribe. With newsgroups, which are not based on e-mail, the reader has to go to a particular place in order to read the materials and post replies. Until recently, specific software "newsreaders" were required to gain access to newsgroups; today, almost all of them are available on the Internet and need nothing more than the browser you already have. There are more than 100,000 from which to choose, according to newsgroups.com. Newsgroups have seen a burst in popularity since being adopted and promoted by services such as GoogleGroups and YahooGroups. You'll sometimes see them referred to as "moderated forums."

Because of the costs—in time, if nothing else—of maintaining an electronic mailing list, some list owners have moved their discussion groups to the Web (we'll point out some of them) and this trend is likely to continue. Because they were identified with popular lists before their Web migration, they are included in the collection that follows later in this chapter.

JOURNALISTIC USES OF MAILING LISTS

Let's explore some of the journalistic reasons to try these e-mail groups.

Search for Expert Sources. Reporters can send e-mail to a mailing list and ask for contacts and information on a particular story. There are lists for virtually every topic, from the environment and higher education to crime and politics.

Searching for "Regular People" Sources. Reporters also can e-mail the list looking for people who will help put a face on a feature or enterprise story. Let's say you are writing a feature on the trend in home beer brewing. You could subscribe to one of the home brewers' listservs (BEER-L or HOMEBREW) and send a query asking for home brewers in your area. It is amazing how specific some of these lists can get. For instance, not only are there dozens of discussion groups for jazz aficionados, but there is one devoted exclusively to an ongoing dialogue on the music of the late jazz trumpeter Miles Davis. A favorite on the obscurity scale is the "Star Trek from a Jewish Cultural Religious Perspective (TREK-COCHAVIM)" list. But treat the responses with the same caution as an unsolicited e-mail from an unknown source. You need to verify that the potential sources are indeed who they claim to be.

Listening In. Good reporters eavesdrop. We listen to conversations among schoolteachers before the school board meeting. We perk up as lawyers chat at the courthouse. We catch snippets of discussions among cops at the station house. We listen to neighbors complaining at the grocery store, dry cleaners, and neighborhood bar. And that's a good thing. That is in part how we find new stories on our beats.

Discussion groups are another way to "listen in" on conversations. Reporters can subscribe to lists in their topic area and "listen" to the conversations by monitoring the e-mail exchanges (this is referred to as "lurking" in Internet parlance). But while hanging around to get a sense of the issues and tone of the group is fine, spying and quoting without asking permission are not. If the group looks worthwhile, introduce yourself and state your objectives.

When one of the authors was researching Lyme disease, newsgroups were among the few places where she could gain context about the complexities of the disease and the controversies that surrounded its treatment.

Professional Development. There are dozens of journalism-related mailing lists with ongoing discussions on everything from computer-assisted reporting to newsroom ethics. Joining one or more of the groups can expose you to new reporting techniques, story ideas, upcoming contests or programs, or perhaps just let you vent about a recent ethical dilemma or newsroom frustration.

WARNINGS

A few things to think about before you sign up for any mailing lists:

Weed through the Garbage. As with so much of what's on the Internet, an overwhelming majority of things you will find on mailing lists are journalistically worthless. Discussion groups can be sidelined by endless chitchat, mindless bickering, off-topic discussions, people who like to "hear" themselves talk, and those who clearly have way too much time on their hands. We marvel at the "threads" (a thread refers to multiple messages posted in response to a single post) that can develop when members discuss how the discussion has gone off-point. In such cases, the first message—the one that was deemed off-point in the first place—is followed by an avalanche of e-mail responses agreeing emphatically with the argument while apparently oblivious to the irony that they are prolonging the very practice they are criticizing. Nevertheless, despite such troubled outbursts, a small sliver of worthwhile material is often exceptional and worth the price of trudging through some muck. Getting to know the makeup and tone of the group you join can ward off much wasted time. Much of the material in this book has been culled over the years from productive journalism-related mailing lists.

One at a Time. Subscribing to more than one mailing list at a time is a sure way of quickly getting turned off by this part of the Internet. Some mailing lists get heavy traffic, with dozens of messages each day. Signing up for multiple lists without scouting them first will surely swamp you with unfocused e-mail.

■ ■ ■ ■ ■ ▬▬▬▬▬▬▬▬▬▬▬▬▬▬▬▬▬▬▬▬▬▬▬▬▬▬▬▬▬▬

BOX 10.1

Mark Schleifstein of the New Orleans Times Picayune *describes how his use of Internet discussion groups helped him report a series on oceans that won the 1997 Pulitzer Prize for Public Service Reporting.*

In December 1994, I wrote a simple paragraph that set in motion the biggest reporting project I've ever been involved with.

My editors had come to me and asked for ideas about projects for the coming year. I glanced through my list of story ideas in my computer and found this note at the very bottom: "The fisheries beat no longer exists. It's covered by a variety of people when a story comes up, but no one spends all their time messing around with it anymore."

The note had been sent to me by an editor several years ago when I asked whether the suburban reporter who had been covering fisheries could pick up a story I was too busy for. I thought about that note, and about my own reporting on habitat-related issues involving Louisiana's wetlands, and wrote the following: "Seafood: We need to do a major take-out on how the rapidly declining stocks of a variety of seafood species, ranging from redfish to shrimp to sea trout, are affecting the state. This is a huge story that we've covered poorly on a daily basis, inasmuch as seafood is the third or fourth largest industry in the state. I see this as a bells-and-whistles project."

I sent the note to my editor and forgot about it.

Two weeks later, he was back at my desk. "Well, you're the project."

The editors had met and decided to team me with three people: John McQuaid, our Washington correspondent, who has quite a bit of experience covering environmental issues, both in Congress and during a two-year stint as our Central American correspondent; Bob Marshall, our nationally respected outdoors writer, who also writes regularly for *Field and Stream* magazine; and photographer Ted Jackson, whose expertise is capturing both complicated people stories and wildlife stories on film.

Trying to keep track of what we were doing—and keep us on track—was Political Editor Tim Morris.

There was only one problem: Was there really a story in fish? The four of us were told to find out—fast.

We called a number of scientists, fisheries experts, biologists, wetlands experts, and politicians. Ironically, they all gave us similar answers.

"Problem? There's no problem. Management is working. We learned our lesson in the Gulf of Mexico from the collapse of commercial fisheries in New England and Alaska. In 20 years, we'll still have enough fish to keep both commercial fishers and recreational anglers happy."

But when we then asked, "What about wetlands loss? What happens if Louisiana continues to lose 25 square miles of wetlands a year?" the answers changed.

"Oh, wetlands loss. Well, if nothing's done, in 20 years there won't be any commercial amounts of fish in the Gulf."

We knew we had a story.

Now, all we had to do was learn everything we could about fish as fast as we could.

As it turned out, we all leaned on the Internet to speed up that process.

Producing our series was a lesson in the value of e-mail as a source of sources, both people and documents. For me, using the Net is an intuitive process. I tend to treat Web sites and e-mail the same way I treat the remote control for my television: I switch around a lot until I find something that interests me, and then settle down to study.

I figured one of the places to start our search for information was to find listservs that dealt with fisheries issues.

When we began our project, America Online had its own searchable list of listservs, so I started there, although today there are several Internet sites that serve the same purpose. I typed in the word *Fisheries* and checked what turned up, and then used other words, like *ocean* and *habitat* and *wetland*, to expand my choices. Several listservs seemed to cover subjects dealing with fisheries. Here are some examples:

AQUA-L is a list for aquaculture businessmen and scientists. I met Bob Rosenberry, the publisher of *Shrimp News International,* on this list. His publication, aimed at shrimp farmers worldwide, provided me with quite a few leads to track down the spread of Taura, a virus that kills farmed shrimp in the United States and around the world.

BENTHOS is devoted to organisms that live on the bottom of the sea. This list proved useful in my research on the effects of the Dead Zone on the bottom of the Gulf of Mexico. The Dead Zone, an area of water that some years is 7,000 square miles in size and stretches from the Mississippi River's mouth to the Texas border, is very low in oxygen content. Fish and shrimp avoid the area, much to the chagrin of fishers.

FISHFOLK is a discussion of social science and fisheries, used by sociologists, anthropologists, and economists. John used this list to gather quite a bit of information about the effects of a system called "individual transferable quotas" that was being considered as a tool for limiting the number of fishers on both the East and West coasts. John also met his wife—an anthropologist who worked at Woods Hole Oceanographic Institute—through the list.

INFOTERRA is an environmentalist-oriented worldwide list that proved quite useful over the past year in our coverage of issues involving gold mining in Indonesia by Freeport-McMoRan, a Fortune 500 company based in New Orleans. We were able to track rumors involving the Bre-X gold mine scam on this list, because it is used by quite a few NGOs (nongovernmental organizations) dealing with indigenous peoples.

John and I started signing up for a number of the lists.

I already was a member of SEJ-L, the Society of Environmental Journalists listserv, as well as CARR-L and NICAR-L, all of which proved useful during the project.

After we signed up for several lists, we sat back and *lurked,* a term describing a subscriber who receives messages, but doesn't participate in the discussion.

We soon learned that each of these lists had different purposes and different members. Some had their own internal political battles going on. Some were in the midst of flame wars. Others were moderated. With the fish lists, we soon found ourselves inundated with information.

On FISHFOLK, for instance, sociologists and biologists and icthyologists were discussing the effects of overfishing on specific fisheries.

An official with the Congressional Research Service was posting a weekly summary of fisheries news he gathered for congressional leaders. That alone was worth the price of admission, as it provided us with valuable leads on everything from the shooting war that broke out between Spain and Canada over fishing rights for turbot, a type of halibut found off the coast of Greenland, to fights between fishers and shrimp farm owners in Thailand and Ecuador. As it turned out, Spanish and Canadian fisheries bureaucrats debated the great Turbot War on the list as it was playing out on the high seas.

On AQUA-L, I began learning about the efforts shrimp farmers were making to fight a variety of viruses, including using different chemicals and antibiotics, and changing varieties of shrimp. Salmon farmers, who raise their fish in cages, were discussing the best feeds and whether fecal matter from their caged fish were causing environmental problems.

We soon ventured out of lurk phase, and began asking questions. Some questions we posted to the list. John asked whether scientists saw a use for chaos theory in developing management plans for Atlantic fisheries. I asked for help in understanding the effects of the release of farmed salmon on wild salmon populations. We both sent out questions aimed at finding fishers or fish farmers or potential locations for our field trips. Other questions we sent to individual list participants, asking for a copy of a particular scientific paper they were discussing or for further information about a particular subject.

Oh, one other thing. The day "Oceans of Trouble" began running, I put out a note on the listservs we were using, thanking people for their help. That night and the next morning, I was literally able to watch the message move around the globe as I received responses time zone by time zone requesting copies of the series.

Digests. Some lists offer the option of receiving daily or weekly "digests" instead of as-people-reply mailings. If the list regularly kicks out dozens of messages a day, this can be a boon. The downside is that you miss out on the immediacy of the discussion.

Separate Mailing List Mail. Most e-mail programs allow users to "filter" mail into separate folders. If you have only one e-mail account, it is advisable to filter the mail from lists into a folder separate from your other mail. If you have more than one account, you may want to have one just for mailing list correspondence.

Not for Daily Deadlines. Like ProfNet, mailing lists are not practical for deadline reporting. Confine the use of discussion groups to enterprise projects.

Quick Hits. While lists are not reliable for daily deadlines, some exceptional lists pride themselves on quick answers. NEWSLIB, for news librarians, makes saves throughout the day as members put up urgent requests for information or material. For them, the list is clearly a professional tool.

Verify Sources. As is the case with single-point e-mail contacts, you cannot be guaranteed that people on the list are who they claim to be. If you are going to pursue potential sources from a mailing list, first verify their identities.

JOURNALISM MAILING LISTS

These are some of the more popular journalism discussion groups available via e-mail. Many of the lists carry related job postings and opportunities. Following each entry is a description of how to subscribe to the list, a process that is explained in more detail later in the chapter (see The Mechanics of Mailing Lists).

General Journalism Topics

Reporting. IRE-L, a mailing list operated by Investigative Reporters and Editors at the University of Missouri School of Journalism, is one of the best journalism mailing lists. With about 1,300 subscribers, it is also among the most popular. Subscribers exchange and debate various reporting tips, techniques and story ideas. Send e-mail

To: listserv@lists.missouri.edu
Message: subscribe IRE-L (your name)

General Journalism. The Society of Professional Journalists, the nation's oldest journalism organization, moved its popular SPJ-L list to its Web site where discussion boards have taken its place. Many regional chapters maintain lists, however (contact each chapter individually). Some of the forums focus on diversity, ethics, international reporting and general journalism. Visit www.spj.org/mb-index.asp. SPJ has about 10,000 members.

Today's Word on Journalism. A journalism saying is selected by Utah State University's Ted Pease and e-mailed daily (except for summers and weekends) to about 1,600 "volunteers." To subscribe, send SUBSCRIBE WORD to tpease@cc.usu.edu.

Computer-Assisted Reporting

NICAR-L. National Institute of Computer-Assisted Reporting List.

To: listserv@lists.missouri.edu
subscribe NICAR-L (your name)

CARR-L. Computer-Assisted Reporting and Research List.

> To: listserv@listserv.louisville.edu
> subscribe CARR-L (your name)

CENSUS-L. This list focuses on Census and mapping issues. Fill out the form at

> http://lists.ire.org/mailman/listinfo/census-l

NEWSLIB. News Librarians mailing list; international membership.

> To: lyris@listserv.unc.edu
> In the body, write: subscribe newslib. Clear your signature.

INTCAR-L. Internationally Oriented Computer-Assisted Reporting List.

> To: listserv@listserv.american.edu
> subscribe INTCAR-L (your name)

Beats

Business Beat. The Society of American Business Editors and Writers operates the SABEW mailing list.

> To: listserv@webworldinc.com
> subscribe SABEW (your name)

Cops and Crime. Criminal Justice Journalists operates CCR.

> To: CCR-on@mail.list.com
> (no message)

Higher Education. The National Education Writers Association operates HigherEd-L for EWA members only. The Web site is www.ewa.org.

Schools. EWA-L, primarily for reporters covering kindergarten through 12th grade, also is for EWA members only.

Environment. The Society of Environmental Journalists (www.sej .org) runs several private mailing lists for members only (more than 1,000). The Knight Center for Environmental Journalism runs KNIGHTLINE. Fill out the form at http://list.msu.edu/cgi-bin/ wa?SUBED1=knightline&A=1.

Science. NASW-TALK, the National Association of Science Writers List, is one of eight lists for the group's more than 2,400 members. Visit www.nasw.org/listservs/subscribe.htm.

Science Freelancing. NASW also runs a science journalism list for free-lance science writers. Visit www.nasw.org/listservs/subscribe.htm.

Children and Families. The Casey Journalism Center on Children and Families (www.cjc.umd.edu) runs CHILDRENSBEAT.

> To: listserv@umdd.umd.edu
> subscribe CHILDRENSBEAT (your name)

International Reporting. CORREX-L is a discussion group for foreign correspondents.

> To: majordomo@true.net
> subscribe CORREX-L (your name)

Religion. The Religion Newswriters Association (www.rna.org) maintains mailing lists for members only.

Specialties around the Newsroom

Investigative Reporters. IRE-Plus. Another list run by Investigative Reporters and Editors, this one devoted exclusively to investigative reporting techniques and projects. Members only. See www.ire.org/membership/listserv.html.

Copy Editors. The American Copy Editors Society (www.copydesk.org) has replaced its mailing list with a discussion board. An RSS feed is available, however. Paste this into your reader: www.copydesk.org/discussionboard/phpBB2/rss.php.

COPYEDITING-L, run by another organization (www.copyediting-l .info), is available at http://listserv.indiana.edu/archives/copyediting-l.html or by sending e-mail

> To: listserv@listserv.indiana.edu
> Message: subscribe copyediting-l Firstname Lastname

Editorial Writers. NCEW-L is a closed list run by the National Conference of Editorial Writers (www.ncew.org/).

Photographers. NPPA-L, run by the National Press Photographers Association List, is now a discussion board: www.nppa.org/news_and_events/discussions/forum/index.php.

Freelance Writers. Contact the Washington Independent Writers (http://washwriter.org/) with regard to WIW-L, a moderated discussion list.

Katim Touray runs FREELANCE-JOURNALISTS, an unmoderated list for freelancers (see also alt.journalism.freelance).

> To: majordomo@mlists.net
> Message: subscribe freelance-journalists firstname lastname

The Editorial Freelancers Association (www.the-efa.org) has a listserv for members.

Online Journalism

Online News. ONA TALK is an e-mail discussion list for members of the Online News Association. Visit http://journalists.org/mailman/listinfo/talk_journalists.org.

ONLINE-NEWS is run by the Poynter Institute. Visit http://talk.poynter.org/cgi-bin/lyris.pl?enter=online-news&text_mode=&lang=english.

FOIA and Press Law

Freedom of Information. FOI-L is the mailing list of the National Freedom of Information Coalition.

> To: listserv@listserv.syr.edu
> subscribe FOI-L (your name)

Press Law Updates. The Reporters Committee for Freedom of the Press' News Media Update. This is not a discussion group, but provides subscribers with e-mailed biweekly reports on laws and rulings affecting journalists. It is also available as a podcast. Visit www.rcfp.org/.

Broadcast Regulation. COMLAW-L, focusing on mass communications law, and PUBUTILSTELCOM-L, for legislation affecting public utilities and telecommunications, are run by the American Association of Law Schools. For subscription links, visit www.washlaw.edu/subject/communication.html.

Journalism Issues

Journalism Ethics. The Society of Professional Journalists runs SPJ-ETHICS.

> To: majordomo@dworkin.wustl.edu
> Message: subscribe SPJ-ETHICS (your e-mail address)

JOURNETHICS is a much smaller discussion group on journalism ethics.

> To: listproc@lists.missouri.edu
> subscribe JOURNETHICS

Diversity. The National Association of Black Journalists (www.nabj.org/) in 1997 became the first minority journalism group to create a mailing list.

> To: listserv@umdd.umd.edu
> subscribe NABJ (your name)

The Asian American Journalists Association maintains a listserv for members. Visit www.aaja.org/.

The South Asian Journalists Association maintains several open e-mail lists. To subscribe, visit http://saja.org/contact/emaillists.html.

Unity, Journalists of Color, maintains discussion forums at www.unityjournalists.org/forums/index.php.

The Society of Professional Journalists maintains a public discussion board on diversity issues at www.spj.org/mb-topic.asp?res=7 as well as The Whole Story, a collection of diversity resources.

The Native American Journalists Association (www.naja.org) runs a listserv for members. RezNetNews (www.reznetnews.org/) is a related student-run site for "news and viewz."

Global News Media. The International Journalists Network (www.ijnet.org) publishes a weekly e-mailed bulletin and runs discussion groups on a wide range of forums. Its Web site has sections in English, Arabic, Spanish, Portuguese and Persian.

Broadcast Journalism

ShopTalk. Subscribers receive a daily e-mailed newsletter about the TV news industry. To subscribe or read it online, visit www.tvspy.com/shoptalk.cfm.

Radio and Television. RTVJ-L is run by the Radio-Television Journalism Division of the Association for Education in Journalism and Mass Communication (but it's for professionals as well as academics).

> To: majordomo@majordomo.umt.edu
> Message: subscribe rtvj-l (email address) (My Real First Name
> My Real Last Name)

A list for broadcasters in the United States and Canada is run by the South Asian Journalists Association (one needn't be South Asian). Subscribe at www.saja.org/contact/emaillists.html.

Television, Radio and Cable. For the Broadcast Discussion List, send e-mail

> To: listserv@listserv.unl.edu
> Message: subscribe BRDCST-L

IRE's Broadcast List. IREBC-L. To subscribe, fill out the form at http://lists.ire.org/mailman/listinfo/irebc-l.

Student Journalism

The Society of Professional Journalists took its many campus-based mailing lists to the Web where they became 12 regional discussion boards. There is also a general forum for all students and student issues at www.spj.org/mb-topic.asp?res=11.

College Media Advisers. CMA-L is open to journalists interested in college student media. To subscribe, visit https://lists.latech.edu/mailman/listinfo/cma-l. Archives are available at https://lists.latech.edu/mailman/private/cma-l/.

Journalism Education

Journalism Educators. More than 500 members keep this list active and practical. Send e-mail

> To: listserv@cmich.edu
> Message: subscribe JOURNET-L

Public Affairs Reporting. The IRE-EDU mailing list serves as a forum for journalism educators specializing in public affairs, investigative or computer-assisted reporting. Members only; visit www.ire.org/membership/listserv.html.

More Journalism Educators. JEANET is based in Australia. To apply for a subscription, visit http://mailinglists.uow.edu.au/mailman/listinfo/jeanet.

Journalism History. This discussion list for the history of journalism and mass communication posts recent list messages to its Web site here: www.h-net.msu.edu/~jhistory/. Discussion logs are searchable by month, author, thread and subject. To subscribe, visit www.h-net.msu.edu/lists/subscribe.cgi?list=Jhistory.

Editing Professors. Begun by Frank Fee at Ohio University, the group has a new home at Deborah Gump's editteach.org. Send e-mail to edprof@editteach.org or visit the site for a subscription form.

> www.editteach.org

FINDING MAILING LISTS

There are several searchable lists of mailing lists on the Web, although, like all other Internet search tools, none is comprehensive. They include:

CataList. L-Soft, which operates the Listserv system, has a database of more than 53,260 public Listserv mailing lists. Go to www.lsoft.com/lists/listref.html or www.lsoft.com/catalist.html

Tile.net. Lists from other operators, including Majordomo and Listproc, are included in this database. The lists are searchable alphabetically by name, description and domain.

> http://tile.net/lists/

Archivum.info. This is a growing archive site for international mailing lists.

> http://archivum.info/index_mails.html.

H-Net Editors Directory. Listservs, primarily academic and having to do with the humanities and social sciences, are linked in this collection.

> www.h-net.msu.edu/people/editors/

ListTool. This site organizes lists by topic and is searchable by key-word. You can easily request e-mailed information on each list included.

www.listtool.com/categories.html

THE MECHANICS OF MAILING LISTS

The Address. To use mailing lists you have to understand a bit about how they function. There are three things needed to operate a mail-ing list—the name of the list, the name of the computer system that is hosting the list, and the type of system that operates the list (such as Listserv, Listproc or Majordomo). When you want to tell the computer system something—such as to sign you up, drop you from the list or provide information about who is on the list—you need to send a com-mand to the computer. The way to contact the computer is to send an e-mail. The portion of the e-mail address before the @ sign must be the type of system (Listserv, etc.). The part after the @ symbol must be the computer host address.

When you want to send a note to the membership of the list, then the first part of the e-mail address must be the name of the list and the sec-ond part the computer host address. This seems fairly straightforward, but it is easy to send a message intended for the list members mistak-enly to the computer (which the computer will bounce back to you), or conversely to send a command intended for the computer to the list members (which will invariably lead to subscribers smugly pointing out the errors of your ways). Just remember, the last part of the address is al-ways the computer host. When you want to write to the list, send to the list name. When you want to tell the computer to do something, write to the computer system. Here is an example for the popular mailing list CARR-L (Computer-Assisted Research & Reporting). The name of the list is CARR-L, the system is Listserv, and the computer host address is
listserv.louisville.edu
To send any command to the computer, type in the Send To box:
listserv@ulkyvm.louisville.edu
To send a message to fellow list members, type in the Send To box:
CARR-L@listserv.louisville.edu

Subscribing. Although many lists now provide a Web-based subscrip-tion form, the old way of subscribing still holds true in many cases. In the Send To command box, type in the name of the mailing list type (e.g., Listserv), then an @ symbol followed by the computer host address. Leave the Cc, Subject and Attachment lines blank and move to the text portion of the screen. Use the same procedure when sending any command to the computer. If you are signing up on a Listserv or Listproc system, write in the text box:

> subscribe (name of list) (your full name)

For Majordomo, write:

> subscribe (list name) (your e-mail address)

Signing Off. To get off a mailing list in all three systems, set up your e-mail address as detailed above, then write in the text:

> unsubscribe (list name)

Sending Messages. To send a message to the list members, type in the Send box:

> listname@computerhostaddress

Before crafting a message, spend a moment thinking of a subject line that is going to catch the eye of readers. This is critical. Often mail list subscribers get so many messages they may not even open up every message, let alone read each one carefully. Think of the subject lines as story slugs on a wire service.

At the Associated Press, writing catchy slugs was an art form because we knew wire editors would be more likely to open up and read stories that had compelling slugs. Subject lines that say "In Need Of Help" probably are not going to get much response. Craft the subject line around the topic of your question or comment.

Replying to Messages. There is nothing more embarrassing than wanting to respond to an individual on the list but sending the message to the entire list instead. Remember, if you hit the "reply" button, the message will be sent to the entire list, not just the person who originated the message. Instead, look at the e-mail address in the "From" line at the top of the original e-mail, and then write a new e-mail using that address if you want to reply to just that person and not the entire list. Furthermore, if you are posting a query for a story, you should specify that you would like respondents to write back to you directly, rather than to the list.

Other Commands. There are other useful commands for each mailing list system, including temporarily stopping a list, obtaining a list of subscribers, getting a digest of messages and getting message indexes. Once you sign up for a list, you will receive a document that details the various commands. Save this document for future use.

Although lists of commands are available online, it can be difficult to know which version your mailing list server is using and the commands can vary. Some helpful lists will automatically send you command information at regular intervals once you're a member. These Mailing List Gurus pages list common commands:

For Listserv: http://lists.gurus.com/listserv.html
For Listproc: http://lists.gurus.com/listproc.html
For Majordomo: http://lists.gurus.com/majordomo.html
For Lyris: http://lists.gurus.com/lyris.html

JOURNALISTIC USES OF NEWSGROUPS

Reporters can use newsgroups for the same reasons as listservs: finding sources and listening in on particular issues. But while mailing lists (which are targeted to narrow interest areas) are best for contacting expert sources, newsgroups excel in helping you find "real people" interested in more general topics. The earliest newsgroups, formed before the Internet was popular, were distributed through a system known as Usenet, which depended on multiple servers retaining a "cache" of messages for a limited amount of time. The servers "communicated" with each other through one-to-one transfers of accumulated information. Although the vast amount of group discussion now takes place on the Internet using network technology, it is important to know how Usenet groups operate and where to find them. Many newsgroups have archived their discussions, making them fruitful targets for investigative reporters; the records can reach back decades.

NEWSGROUP STRUCTURE

Newsgroups are organized by large categories, or hierarchies, such as science, recreation or computers. Those categories are broken down by topic and subtopic, divided by dots. For instance, sci.environment.waste.

There are eight major Usenet hierarchies:

Comp.	News.
Rec.	Sci.
Soc.	Talk.
Misc.	Humanities

There are dozens of other hierarchies. The most popular is "alt," which covers "alternative" topics (including erotica: be warned). A master list of hierarchies is located at www.magma.ca/~leisen/mlnh/index.html.

FINDING AND SEARCHING NEWSGROUPS

By far the easiest and quickest way to locate newsgroups is to go through GoogleGroups, which also offers a search option for what may be the largest Usenet archive available (it incorporates the DejaNews database, which goes back to 1981 posts). Go directly to the advanced search function at http://groups.google.com/advanced_search?q=&.

> *Tile.net.* Newsgroups are searchable by index, description and newsgroup hierarchy.
>
> > http://tile.net/news/
>
> *Archivum.info.* This is a growing archive site for international newsgroups.
>
> > http://archivum.info/index_news.html
>
> AOL Search Newsgroups
>
> > http://site.aol.com/netfind/newsgroups.html

USING A GROUP AS A WORKING TOOL

Groups are helpful for more than research. Reporters working together on a project can easily set up a collaborative "space" online for sharing information, creating and monitoring a "to-do" list and drafting and revising stories. It can also be a handy space for linking to relevant articles, multimedia, sources, etc. Google Groups can set up your group in minutes and allows you to restrict access to invited members and mask it from search engines and the public directory.

> http://groups.google.com/

Yahoo Groups also provides an easy program but, at the time of this writing, does not offer privacy. If you want others to find you—if you're urging people to post comments for a story, for example—this might be perfect. Find, browse, or start your own at

> http://groups.yahoo.com/

CHAPTER 11

WEBLOGS

The earliest blogs, in the 1990s, tended to be lists of new Web sites or bits of information to be shared with small groups of like-minded people. Slashdot's "News for Nerds" was an early entrant in the field in fall 1997. With the 1999 release of Blogger, a Web-based program that made it easy to create blogs, all that changed. The wild popularity of blogs was seen in a proliferation of personal sites, giving rise to the association of blogs with diaries and commentary.

Some of the uses to which blogs have been put made them nearly synonymous with unchecked opinion, informality, spontaneity and inaccuracy. Since then, many blogs have become news sources, reporting tools and vehicles of credible analysis. Many blogs provide journalists with reliable, timely and valuable information. The trick is knowing which ones they are and how to find them. With more than 84 million blogs (tracked by Technorati in June 2007), that can take some doing.

Recently, blogs have become a tool of choice for the mojo (mobile journalist) and they've distinguished themselves as ways to post short bursts of information in a hurry when people need it most, as in a disaster. Hurricane Katrina blogs formed a vital role in saving lives, reuniting families and creating a cumulative and very human record of a complex event. In 2007, for the first time, the U.S. federal government issued bloggers press credentials, a right won by the Media Bloggers Association.

BLOG MECHANICS

Most Recent First. Blogs are compiled in reverse chronological order, which makes the time-and-date stamp that appears on each entry a key element. Beyond a certain point, blog posts are stored in an archive that is accessible from the home page of the blog.

Permalinks. Blogs are all about links, whether they're to other blogs, news sources, multimedia productions or entries within the blog itself. The latter is called a permalink and it's usually found at the end of an entry (or "post"). If you save this link, you will be able to return to that specific entry without having to search through the entire blog. If you're without something to write it down or you're not using your own computer, e-mail the permalink to yourself for later retrieval.

Comments. At the end of a post, there's usually a link that invites feedback or elaboration. Click on it and a text window will appear in which you can type your comment. Others will be offered the chance to react to your comment as well.

Tags. These are topical notations that let you search for topic-specific entries. These, along with headlines and text, are "read" by many search engine crawlers.

Trackbacks. These are feedback mechanisms that let blogs "talk" to one another. They let other blogs "know" when they've been quoted or cited, and let readers easily navigate between the blogs for a fuller discussion.

Blogrolls. Think of a rollcall and you'll have the idea: blogrolls are lists of links to other blogs. They're usually found in the sidebar (rail) of the blog.

BLOG TYPES

Blogs tend to be topical, which just means they usually have a focus. That can be on the blogger, as in a personal diary (MerandaWrites.com); an interest, such as cooking (chocolateandzucchini.com); a political focus (redstate.com); or a reporting beat, as with Kevin Sites' coverage of "hotzones" around the world for Yahoo.news. In the journalism world, few blogs are more famous than Romenesko, which chronicles the inner workings of the news biz.

Blogs aren't just text. Genre spinoffs include photoblogs, videoblogs (vlogs) and audioblogs. They can be written by one person or many. Notable collaborative blogs include DailyKos and HuffingtonPost. Now that we've briefly explored what blogs are, let's look at a few ways to find them

FINDING BLOGS

Technorati. Tracks more than 84 million blogs (June 2007). Get an overview with its WTF (What's the Fire?) summaries.

www.technorati.com/

Google Blog Search. Indexes all blogs that publish a site feed, not just from Google-owned blogger blogs. Thirty-five languages. Searches return both individual posts and entire blogs, when relevant. Can get updates sent to your news aggregator. For more details, see www.google.com/help/about_blogsearch.html or go directly to http://blogsearch.google.com/?tab=wb.

IceRocket Blogs. Searches within blogs and finds blogs by their tags. Calls itself the "real-time Web, organized by bloggers."

www.icerocket.com/

Tailrank is a memetracker: it reports blog entries based on how popular they are and is in constant fluctuation.

http://tailrank.com/

Cyberjournalist List of J-Blogs. Founder Jon Dube, then at the *Charlotte Observer*, was the first to blog a news event for a newspaper.

www.cyberjournalist.net/cyberjournalists.php

Retired. If you're exploring blog search engines or working from an out-of-date reference, you'll likely see links to Blogdex. It was a popular tool that ranked blogs by how often they were cited by other blogs, but it's been offline since May 2006.

Luck of the Draw. If you go to the home page of Blogger.com, you'll see a constant feed of blogs as they're updated. Click on any one to sample it. Blogger provides its blog pages with a "next blog" feature in the tool bar. It serves up what appear to be random choices. Be warned: blogs cover all sorts of topics, some offensive, and there's no guarantee you won't come across some of them.

www.blogger.com

Local and Hyperlocal. If you're on an issue beat, wide-ranging blogs are terrific. On a local story, though, you need to get close to home. Check out one of the successful placeblogs: www.H2Otown.info, which serves Watertown, Mass. Finding regional blogs can be a boon, and it's getting easier all the time. Try Placeblogger.com (where you can search by locality and ZIP), local newspaper sites, MySpace and the blogrolls of any blog from that area. There's a growing regional directory on Blogflux: http://dir.blogflux.com/cat/regional.html and Outside.in (http://outside.in/news/bloggiest_neighborhoods.php) has neighborhoods by ZIP.

GATHERING AND ORGANIZING BLOGS

Blogs in all their forms (text, video, etc.) are created with software that allows them to be sent to you in various ways. The easiest way to keep track of your subscriptions is to collect them in one place, which you can do using an aggregator. This can be done by supplying the aggregator with the blog's url (address) or by clicking a "subscribe" or "RSS" button included on more and more blogs (see Chapter 7). Some feed gatherers let you install tools (bookmarklets) on your browser for instant subscriptions. These options are likely to increase. Here are some of the best aggregators at present:

> *Technorati.* Download the bookmarklet for your browser's toolbar and you'll be able to add any blog. Let Technorati track your favorites, which you can organize with tags for easy searching.
>
> http://technorati.com/
>
> *Bloglines.* Lets you save selected text from Web pages into a section called Clippings. Create a personal page. Track newsgroups, e-newsletters, podcasts, blogs and more in nine languages. Search billions of articles through Ask.com technology. For other options, visit
>
> www.bloglines.com/
>
> *Feedster.* This site's strength is in breaking news and current information. It tracks some 30 million online sites, including blogs and news services. Search billions of blog posts in "real time" by keyword or surf the latest entries in Feedster's content channels: technology, life experiences, sports, celebrity gossip and politics.
>
> www.feedster.com
>
> *LinkRoll.* Free public-only link-blogging service that will send links to blogs and podcasts to your RSS reader. Searchable. Modeled on del.icio.us.
>
> www.linkroll.com/index.php
>
> *Digg.* Seen the Digg icon next to blog posts and news stories? Promoted as "digital democracy," Digg inhales, publishes and ranks the vast number of stories, posts and podcasts sent its way by readers. Can you Digg it? Turns out you can, which is helpful for reporters. Once you've registered, you can keep a history of everything you Digg.
>
> www.digg.com/

EVALUATING BLOGS

The best way to know the tenor and integrity of a blog is to read it in depth, but failing the time to do that, there are several methods to employ. First, check it out online. See what others have to say. Many blogs have been reviewed in credible publications. Second, check the company it keeps. Most blogs publish a home-page list of blog links called a blogroll. Check them. Are all the blogs from a particular point of view or are they diverse? Are they well written? Do they have credible and interesting blogrolls themselves? Are they active—when was the last post? The one before that? Are the comments, if any, constructive and intelligent or shallow and off-topic? Do a Technorati search and see who links to the blog.

A SELECTION OF USEFUL BLOGS

Although this list is targeted toward journalistic utility, it should give you a good idea of the range of blogs in active production. Technorati reports there are more than 175,000 new blogs detected each day.

Blog Portals—Many Topics

Corante Blogs   www.corante.com/
MSNBC "Blogs, Etc."   www.msnbc.msn.com/id/3032105/
CBSNews
   www.cbsnews.com/stories/2007/01/03/blogs/main2327516.shtml
ABCNews   http://abcnews.go.com/technology/blogs
New York Times   www.nytimes.com/ref/topnews/blog-index.html
Washingtonpost.com   http://blog.washingtonpost.com/
Wall Street Journal   http://online.wsj.com/page/8_0019.html
HuffingtonPost, All the Blogs   www.huffingtonpost.com/theblog/
Slate Blogs+   http://slate.com/
The Blog Report   http://blogreport.salon.com/

Business

Blogspotting   www.businessweek.com/the_thread/blogspotting/
The Key   http://blogs.business2.com/sloan

Education

Education Wonks   http://educationwonk.blogspot.com/

Environment

Treehugger   www.treehugger.com/

Health

World Health Care Blog   http://worldhealthcareblog.org/

HealthLawProf
   http://lawprofessors.typepad.com/healthlawprof_blog/
Health Care Policy and Marketplace Review
   http://healthpolicyandmarket.blogspot.com/
Wall Street Journal Health Blog   http://blogs.wsj.com/health/

Journalism, Media

Romenesko   www.poynter.org/column.asp?id=45
Common Sense Journalism   http://commonsensej.blogspot.com/
First Draft by Tim Porter   www.timporter.com/firstdraft/
Howard Owens   http://howardowens.com/
Innovation in College Media   http://reinventing.collegemedia.org/
Invisible Inkling   www.ryansholin.com/
Cyberjournalist   www.cyberjournalist.net/
Editor's Weblog   www.editorsweblog.org/
Online Journalism   http://onlinejournalismblog.wordpress.com/
The Kicker, Columbia Journalism Review   www.cjr.org/the_kicker/
News Gems: Highlighting the Best of American Journalism
   http://spj.org/blog/blogs/newsgems/
E-Media Tidbits   www.poynter.org/column.asp?id=31
Press Think
   http://journalism.nyu.edu/pubzone/weblogs/pressthink/
Buzz Machine   www.buzzmachine.com/
Media Giraffe Project   http://newshare.typepad.com/mediagiraffe/

Journalism Training

NU Access   http://access.newsu.org/

Language and Editing

The Slot   www.theslot.com
You Don't Say: Language and Usage
   http://blogs.baltimoresun.com/about_language/
News Designer   www.newsdesigner.com/blog/
Page One Today   www.poynter.org/column.asp?id=49

SND Update   www.snd.org/update/
Regret the Error   www.regrettheerror.com/

Law

The Blawg Directory   www.blawg.com/
Media Law: A Blog About Freedom of the Press
 www.legaline.com/medialaw.html
Legal Blog Watch   http://legalblogwatch.typepad.com/
Lessig Blog. Cyberspace rights activist Lawrence Lessig covers copyright, political coverage, culture and more   www.lessig.org/blog/
Law Professors   www.lawprofessorblogs.com/

Miscellaneous

BoingBoing: A Directory of Wonderful Things   www.boingboing.net/
PostSecret: An Ongoing Community Art Project
 http://postsecret.blogspot.com/
Mashable! Social Networking Blog   http://mashable.com/
Chocolate and Zucchini   http://chocolateandzucchini.com/
Flickr Blog   http://blog.flickr.com/
Gizmodo, the Gadget Guide   www.gizmodo.com/

Places

MoleskinCity Blogs   www.moleskinecity.com/jo/index.php
Outside.In What's New
 http://outside.in/news/bloggiest_neighborhoods.php

Politics

Daily Kos   www.dailykos.com/
Swing State Project   www.swingstateproject.com/frontPage.do
CQPolitics   www.cqpolitics.com/
Democratic Party, Kicking Ass   www.democrats.org/blog.html
Taegan Goddard's Political Wire   http://politicalwire.com/
Andrew Sullivan's Daily Dish
 http://andrewsullivan.theatlantic.com/the_daily_dish/

Drudge Report   www.drudgereport.com/
Talking Points Memo   www.talkingpointsmemo.com/
Wonkette   www.wonkette.com

Reporting

The Scoop (Investigative Reporting)   www.thescoop.org/
News Videographer   http://newsvideographer.com/
Extra! Extra! Your Guide to the Latest Investigative Work
   www.ire.org/extraextra/
Public Diplomacy Press and Blog Review
   http://uscpublicdiplomacy.com/index.php/newsroom/
   johnbrown_main
MEMRI Blog (on Middle East reporting)   www.thememriblog.org/

Science

Wired Science   http://blog.wired.com/wiredscience/
Knight Science Journalism Tracker   http://ksjtracker.mit.edu/

Search

Yahoo! Search   www.ysearchblog.com/
John Battelle's Search   http://battellemedia.com/
Search Engine Watch   http://blog.searchenginewatch.com/blog/

Security

No Quarter   http://noquarter.typepad.com/
Secrecy News   www.fas.org/blog/secrecy/
Spy Talk   www.jeffstein.info/
The Bad Guys   www.usnews.com/usnews/news/badguys/
Counterterrorism Blog   http://counterterrorismblog.org/

Sports

Boston Sports Media Watch/Bruce Allen
   http://bostonsportsmedia.com/
Sports Blog Nation   www.sbnation.com/

Transparency in Sport   www.transparencyinsport.org/
HockeyDirt   www.hockeydirt.com/
Off Wing Opinion   www.ericmcerlain.com/offwingopinion/

Technology

TechCrunch   www.techcrunch.com/
Lifehacker   www.lifehacker.com
Slashdot: News for Nerds   http://slashdot.org/

Warblogs/Milblogs

Milblogging.com: "World's Largest Index of Military Blogs"
   http://milblogging.com/
SpouseBuzz: For military spouses   www.spousebuzz.com/

Weblogs from Around the World
(assorted award winners)

Australia/New Zealand: The Breakfast Blog
   http://thebreakfastblog.blogspot.com/
Asia: Tokyo Girl Down Under   http://tokyo-girl.blogspot.com/
African/Middle Eastern: Secret Dubai Diary
   http://secretdubai.blogspot.com/
Latin American: Cooking Diva   www.panamagourmet.blogs.com/
Canadian: Drawn!   www.drawn.ca/
American: Cute Overload   www.cuteoverload.com/
Singapore: It's Raining Noodles (a teen blog)
   http://raining-noodles.blogspot.com/

RESOURCES

Electronic Frontier Foundation's Legal Guide for Bloggers
   http://www.eff.org/bloggers/lg/
Media News   www.mediabistro.com/
Media Bloggers Association   www.mediabloggers.org/node
Online Journalism Review, Readers' Blog Archive
   www.ojr.org/ojr/blog/

WIKIS

These are like next-stage blogs and they're growing in popularity. Wikis are collaborative Web sites where it's possible for anyone viewing the site pages to edit and post entries. Perhaps the most famous wiki is Wikipedia, the volunteer-written encyclopedia that, at last check, contained 7.4 million articles in 253 languages. The collaborative nature of wikis is both their strength and their weakness. They can harness tremendous breadth and expertise, but it's difficult to assess their accuracy. As use of wikis has grown, so has the practice of monitoring their contents and enforcing the editors' standards. Wikipedia, for example, has flagged certain topics for review and imposed delays on updates received from certain computers. It employs a growing staff of editors. Best advice: Get an overview from a wiki and then pursue the story. Here are a few particularly good links to resources and examples.

Wikipedia (English)   http://en.wikipedia.org/wiki/Main_Page

JournaWiki   http://journalism.wikia.com/wiki/Main_Page

WikiFOIA   http://wikifoia.pbwiki.com/

Online Journalism Wikis (tutorials for reporting online)
   http://www.ojr.org/ojr/wiki/

WikiNews   http://en.wikinews.org/wiki/Main_Page

Citizendium   http://en.citizendium.org/wiki/Main_Page

Congresspedia
   http://www.sourcewatch.org/index.php?title=Congresspedia

iBrattleboro Community Brain Trust
   www.ibrattleboro.com/braintrust/index.php/Main_Page

PROFESSIONAL DEVELOPMENT

Over the past 25 years or so, the journalism profession has seen an explosive growth of journalism organizations, institutes and programs designed to help working journalists improve their craft through continuing education programs, workshops and conferences, reporting and writing tools and techniques, fellowships, awards, research on a wide variety of press topics and job listings. As newsroom resources shrank, it became ever more important for journalists to continue learning on their own. Many felt it was a way to take more responsibility for their own careers, to network, and to help strengthen the profession as a whole.

THE BEST JOURNALISM WEB SITES

The information available on the Internet about journalism is so rich it is hard to highlight the best, but the following Web sites are among the most useful for the widest variety of journalists and student journalists.

Romenesko. Formerly known as MediaNews, Jim Romenesko's site is the place where journalists go to get news about the industry—and themselves. Romenesko, who started the site as a hobby and now runs it from the Poynter Institute Web site (see Figure 12.1), provides headlines, blurbs and links to press-related stories and updates the site throughout the day.

www.poynter.org/medianews

Daily Briefing page of the Project for Excellence in Journalism.

www.journalism.org/-dailybriefings

Editor & Publisher online is updated daily.

www.editorandpublisher.com/eandp/-index.jsp

American Journalism Review. AJR's News Sources section (a development of the former NewsLink) provides one of the best hyperlinked

117

FIGURE 12.1   Jim Romenesko's journalism blog at www.poynter.org/medianews

(Reprinted with permission of The Poynter Institute.)

compilations of newspapers, magazines, television networks and affiliates, radio, new/wire services and media companies worldwide. The home page also links to dozens of awards and fellowships available to journalists, an archived index of AJR stories, full-text articles of the current magazine and the State of the American Newspaper project.

www.ajr.org

Investigative Reporters and Editors. IRE's Web site (see Figure 12.2) includes a searchable database of more than 20,000 investigative stories and some 2,000 tip sheets, reporting guides and beat sources. It also offers campaign finance data and sources, a directory of investigative and project reporters worldwide and details on IRE contests, programs and conferences.

www.ire.org

Society of Professional Journalists. SPJ's site is a gateway to *Quill* magazine, a collection of SPJ blogs and discussion boards, Today's Media News, job postings, awards and internships, many resource collections and the Legal Defense Fund and the active SPJ events calendar, among other riches.

www.spj.org

FIGURE 12.2   Home page for IRE.

(Reprinted with permission of Investigative Reporters and Editors, Inc.)

The Poynter Institute for Media Studies. Poynter's weeklong workshops are some of the best journalism educational opportunities available. Poynteronline provides details on those seminars (as well as many others, including Webinars and regional programs) and includes presentations and research from the institute on topics from newspaper management to newsroom diversity. The Institute sponsors numerous blogs exploring issues of importance to journalists. NewsU (www.newsu.org), which offers an expanding roster of online training modules, has many free or inexpensive opportunities where you can explore the art and use of typography, how to produce multimedia projects, handling race and ethnicity, ethical challenges and much more.

www.poynter.org

Reporters Committee for Freedom of the Press. The committee provides some of the most practical tools for reporters, such as the Freedom of Information Act letter generator (p. 38), state laws on open records and public meetings (p. 38), updates on Freedom of Information cases from around the country and a legal defense hotline for journalists.

www.rcfp.org

NEWSROOM SPECIALISTS

Computer-Assisted Reporters. The National Institute for Computer-Assisted Reporting, operated by IRE and the University of Missouri School of Journalism, provides listings of the government databases that can be purchased through NICAR for data analysis projects. There also is information on conferences, training programs and consulting services.

www.nicar.org

Editorial Writers. The National Conference of Editorial Writers Web site features editorial exchanges and critiques, links to online resources for editorial page writers, and NCEW events and programs.

www.ncew.org

Copy Editors. The American Copy Editors Society's Web site is a gateway to numerous resources (including reference links), discussion forums, ACES convention information, editing awards and scholarships, membership news, job banks and links to regional chapters.

www.copydesk.org

News Designers. The Society for News Design is devoted to the design and visual editing of newspapers, magazines and news-oriented Web sites. SND's site includes a job bank, conference news, membership information and resources for news designers, graphic artists, photographers and multimedia reporters—including a popular blog, SND Update. Its SND Quick Courses take training around the country throughout the year and SND co-sponsors multimedia storytelling workshops with ONA.

www.snd.org

Online Journalists. Founded in 1999, the Online News Association has grown to a membership exceeding 1,000. ONA sponsors an annual convention, awards, original research, training sessions (with SND, Associated Press Managing Editors and American Society of News Editors, among others), regional chapter events, online discussion forums, a legal resource center and a bi-weekly newsletter for members.

www.journalist.org

Feature Editors. The American Association of Sunday and Feature Editors sponsors an annual convention and an extensive awards program. AASFE's Web site includes text and video excerpts from the convention, a Flash presentation of feature pages, and a job bank.

www.aasfe.org

Photographers. National Press Photographers Association online provides information on NPPA programs, contests and activities. Its home page features recent award-winning news photos.

www.nppa.org

International Journalists. The International Center for Journalists (formerly the Center for Foreign Journalists) outlines exchange and fellowship programs for U.S. journalists to work abroad and foreign journalists to work in the United States, a database and newsletter on central and eastern European press issues, and information on the center's workshops, seminars, and conferences.

www.icfj.org

Freelance Writers. The National Writers Union, a labor union for freelance writers, has a Web site designed to assist freelancers with information on rights and risks of freelancing and contract advice.

www.nwu.org/nwu

More Freelancers. The American Society of Journalists and Authors is for freelance journalists and authors.

www.asja.org

Magazine Journalists. The Web site of the American Society of Magazine Editors contains news about the magazine industry, ASME's college internship program and its National Magazine Awards.

www.asme.magazine.org/home/

Alternative Journalists. The Association of Alternative Weeklies represents 125 free weekly newspapers in the U.S. and Canada. The Web site includes news about the alternative press, a job bank, and details on the annual convention.

http://aan.org/alternative/Aan/index

Columnists. The National Society of Newspaper Columnists' site includes the group's latest newsletter, information on the convention and the NSNC Hall of Fame.

www.columnists.com

Editorial Cartoonists. The Raleigh, N.C.–based Association of American Editorial Cartoonists has news tidbits about newspaper cartoonists and displays cartoons.

http://editorialcartoonists.com/

Ombudsmen. The Organization of News Ombudsmen provides links to current columns from newspaper ombudsmen around the country as well as to relevant articles and conference coverage.

www.newsombudsmen.org/

BEATS

Education. The Education Writers Association provides a site for reporters on the schools and higher education beats, including Web resources, full-text articles and contest information.

www.ewa.org

Business. The Society of American Business Editors and Writers features the Best in the Business contest, Web links for business reporters, a resumé bank, the Business Journalist newsletter and SABEW conference and program information.

www.sabew.org

Environment. The Society of Environmental Journalists (SEJ) provides linked Web resources, job opportunities and SEJ membership and conference information.

www.sej.org

Science. One of the oldest journalism organizations, the National Association of Science Writers features guides and advice for science writers and convention updates.

www.nasw.org

Children and Families. The Casey Journalism Center on Children and Families offers resources and articles about coverage of disadvantaged children and their families.

casey.umd.edu

Washington Correspondents. The Regional Reporters Association represents Washington correspondents who cover the nation's capital from a local perspective.

www.rra.org

Health Care. The Web site for the Association of Health Care Journalists includes links to information useful for health care reporters.

www.ahcj.umn.edu

Police and Courts. Founded in 1997 at the University of Pennsylvania, the Criminal Justice Journalists group links to examples of excellent police and court reporting and has links to beat resources. The discussion list, Cops and Court Reporters, was reactivated in April 2007.

www.reporters.net/cjj

Statehouse. Capitol Beat: The Association of Capitol Reporters and Editors is a coalition of Statehouse correspondents formed in 1999.

www.capitolbeat.org

Sports. The Web site of the Associated Press Sports Editors includes archives of APSE's newsletters and information on its annual convention.

http://apse.dallasnews.com

Religion. Religion Newswriters Association is one of the oldest journalism groups in the country (it started in 1949). The Web site has information on RNA's contest, annual convention and its mentoring program.

www.rna.org/

Specializations. The Knight Center for Specialized Journalism offers one- and two-week seminars on a wide variety of journalism specialties.

www.knightcenter.umd.edu

JOURNALISM MAGAZINES AND NEWSLETTERS

American Journalism Review, the monthly press critique published by the University of Maryland College of Journalism.

www.ajr.org

Columbia Journalism Review, the monthly press review published by Columbia University Graduate School of Journalism.

www.cjr.org

Online Journalism Review, the Web-only publication from the Annenberg School of Communication at the University of Southern California.

www.ojr.org

Editor & Publisher Interactive, daily online partner of the weekly magazine.

www.mediainfo.com

The American Editor, the online edition of the monthly magazine of the American Society of Newspaper Editors.

http://tae.asne.org

Presstime, the monthly magazine of the Newspaper Association of America.

www.naa.org/home/PressTime.aspx

Nieman Reports, the journal of the Nieman Foundation at Harvard University.

www.nieman.harvard.edu/reports/contents.html

Black Journalism Review, the monthly African-American journalism critique.

www.blackjournalism.com

Communicator, the monthly magazine from the Radio and Television News Directors Association.

www.rtnda.org/communicator/archive.shtml

The Business Journalist, the semi-monthly newsletter of the Society of American Business Writers and editors.

www.sabew.org/newsletter/business-journalist.htm

SEJournal, the quarterly publication of the Society of Environmental Journalists.

www.sej.org/pub/index.htm

Children's Beat, the twice-yearly magazine of the Casey Journalism Center on Children and Families. Free subscriptions are available on request to info@cjc.umd.edu.

The Regional Reporter, the monthly newsletter of the Regional Reporters Association for Washington correspondents.

www.rra.org/newsletter.html

ASPE, the newsletter of the Associated Press Sports Editors.

http://apse.dallasnews.com/

Tracker, the quarterly publication of the Campaign Finance Information Center of Investigative Reporters and Editors.

www.campaignfinance.org/tracker

News Media & the Law, the quarterly magazine of the Reporters Committee for Freedom of the Press.

www.rcfp.org/news/mag

State FOI newsletters. Links to newsletters from around the country are available via the National Freedom of Information Coalition.

http://nfoic.org/resources

Journal of Mass Media Ethics, a quarterly publication focusing on ethics problems in mass communication.

www.jmme.org

Journalism & Mass Communication Educator, a quarterly journal published by the Association for Education in Journalism and Mass Communication.

www.aejmc.org/JMCEfolderD5/JMCE/index.html

Newspaper Research Journal, a quarterly journal published by the Association for Education in Journalism and Mass Communication.

www.newspaperresearchjournal.org/

MINORITY JOURNALISM ORGANIZATIONS

These organizations provide information on newsroom diversity issues and group events, programs and convention information.

National Association of Black Journalists   www.nabj.org
National Association of Hispanic Journalists   www.nahj.org
Asian American Journalism Association   www.aaja.org
National Lesbian & Gay Journalists Association   www.nlgja.org
National Association of Minority Media Executives
    www.namme.org
Unity (coalition of NABJ, NAHJ, AAJA and NAJA)
    www.unityjournalists.org
South Asian Journalists Association   www.saja.org
Native American Journalists Association   www.naja.com

NEWSPAPER MANAGEMENT AND LEADERSHIP

American Society of Newspaper Editors   www.asne.org
Associated Press Managing Editors   www.apme.com
American Press Institute   www.newspaper.org
Newspaper Association of America   www.naa.org
Magazine Publishers of America   www.magazine.org
Newsletter & Electronic Publishers Association   www.newsletters.org
National Newspaper Association   www.nna.org

JOURNALISM RESEARCH

Pew Research Center for the People and the Press
    http://people-press.org
J-Lab: The Institute for Interactive Journalism
    www.j-lab.org/
Joan Shorenstein Center for Press, Politics and Public Policy
    www.ksg.harvard.edu/presspol/index.htm
Annenberg Washington Program in Communications Policy Studies
    www.annenberg.northwestern.edu

Freedom Forum First Amendment Center
  www.firstamendmentcenter.org
Readership Institute   www.readership.org/
Committee to Protect Journalists   www.cpj.org
Project for Excellence in Journalism   www.journalism.org
Committee of Concerned Journalists   www.concernedjournalists.org/
John S. and James L. Knight Foundation   www.knightfdn.org
Association for Education in Journalism and Mass Communication
  www.aejmc.org
Fairness and Accuracy in Reporting   www.fair.org
American Press Institute   www.americanpressinstitute.org
Center for Media and Public Affairs   www.cmpa.com

WOMEN IN JOURNALISM

Journalism and Women Symposium   www.jaws.org
National Federation of Press Women   www.nfpw.org
Association for Women in Communications   www.womcom.org
Association for Women in Sports Media   www.awsmonline.org

BROADCAST JOURNALISM

Radio Television News Directors Association   www.rtnda.org
National Association of Broadcasters   www.nab.org
Shoptalk   www.tvspy.com/shoptalk.cfm
News Blues   www.newsblues.com
NewsLab   www.newslab.org

OTHER JOURNALISM GROUPS

Newseum. The Freedom Forum's Interactive Museum of News is dedicated to journalism and journalists
  www.newseum.org

National Press Club. The Web site provides information about the various NPC events, awards, scholarships and services.

http://npc.press.org

Freedom of Information Coalition. This group is a coalition of various state First Amendment and open government organizations.

http://nfoic.org

The Newspaper Guild-CWA. The home page of the newspaper union includes highlights from the current issue of the *Guild Reporter.*

www.newsguild.org

Newswise www.newswise.com

Pulitzer Prize Organization www.pulitzer.org

COLLEGE AND HIGH SCHOOL JOURNALISM

Student Press Law Center. Includes text of the *SPLC Report.*

www.splc.org

Internships and Job Opportunities. Greig Stewart, the University of Maryland.

www.journalism.umd.edu/intern

Dow Jones Newspaper Fund. Summer internships and training.

www.dowjones.com/newsfund

College Media Advisers. www.collegemedia.org

Journalism Education Association www.jea.org

ASNE's High School Journalism www.highschooljournalism.org

Columbia Scholastic Press Association www.columbia.edu/cu/cspa

National Scholastic Press Association www.studentpress.org/nspa/

Quill & Scroll www.uiowa.edu/~quill-sc

A JOURNALIST'S GUIDE TO THE INTERNET: THE WEB SITE

This book contains hundreds of Internet addresses that can help journalists do their jobs better and faster. Unfortunately, Web addresses change frequently. To take into account the ever-changing nature of the Internet,

Christopher Callahan in early 1998 launched a Web version of "A Journalist's Guide to the Internet." The site, organized by reporting topics such as Politics, Courts and the Law and Records and FOIA, quickly became one of the most popular reporting resources. More than 300 Web sites around the world link to it, including the National Institute for Computer-Assisted Reporting, The *New York Times*, Gannett, Investigative Reporters and Editors, National Press Foundation and Poynter Institute. An updated site is available at http://reporter.umd.edu.

INDEX